Beyond the Beat

A Guide to Success From a Police Officer and Entrepreneur

Brendan Scott Ecker

Copyright © 2023

All rights reserved.

ISBN: 978-1-916787-55-1

All rights reserved. No part of this publication may be reproduced, distributed, or transmitted in any form or by any means, including photocopying, recording, or other electronic or mechanical methods, without the author's prior written permission, except in the case of brief quotations embodied in critical reviews and certain other non-commercial uses permitted by copyright law. For permission requests, please get in touch with the author.

Contents

Dedication 1

Acknowledgments 2

About the Author 4

Author's Note 1

Introduction 6

Chapter 1: What is a Police Officer? What Does It Take to Become One? 18

Chapter 2: Why I Became a Police Officer 23

Chapter 3: How Badly Do You Want It? 44

Chapter 4: Staying Out Of Trouble - Show Me Your Friends….. 52

Chapter 5: Relationships - Be Careful Who You Date 66

Chapter 6: Becoming Financially Literate 81

Chapter 7: Work Like a Cop, But Think Like a Business Owner... 108

Chapter 8: The 3 Paths - It is Important to Know What is and isn't Important 124

Chapter 9: The Police Academy 142

Chapter 10: The State Licensing Exam: Adversity 180

Chapter 11: Getting Hired... 190

Chapter 12: Keeping the Job: FTO (Field Training Officer) 194

Chapter 13: Stay Healthy: Coordinate A Health & Fitness Program 216

Chapter 14: Never Stop Learning - Be Industrious and Be Dynamic 226

Chapter 15: Pay It Forward - Teach & Educate the Next Line of Warriors 230

Sent by the Gods by Brendan Scott Ecker 238

Dedication

My Mother, Jennifer Lyn McKelvie, and to all of my coaches and closest friends.

Acknowledgments

I would like to thank my Mother, Jennifer McKelvie, for being my hero and constantly pushing me to succeed and finish what I started. I learned hard work from her, as I have never seen a woman work harder. Being a single mom is a challenge, and it is extremely difficult (especially with me as your son). I Love you, Mom. You are indeed the greatest role model and mentor a son could have. It was always just us growing up. I will never fail to make you proud and to honor your name. The future generations of the McKelvie and Ecker bloodlines will always remain strong, wealthy, prudent, and powerful because of the lessons you have taught me. Thank you.

I would also like to thank my high school teachers, college professors, and mentors who have played a significant role in my adolescence. If it hadn't been for them,

I would have never become the man I am today. I thank them all for their work in teaching me important lessons, which later allowed this book to come to life. I thank my (true) friends, family members, and especially those of you who are reading this book. Thank you for your support. Thank you all.

I thank any current or retired police officers, correctional officers, soldiers, sailors, veterans, firefighters, EMTs, Nurses, Teachers, and dispatchers who help to keep the peace in a world that is filled with fear, confusion, and chaotic, abstract warfare. Without you, there would be no peace. Without further or do, enjoy, reader. I wish you great success in your journey of becoming a police officer or maybe even an entrepreneur.

Lastly but most importantly, I would like to thank God for allowing this book to be made, as it is my honor to represent and play a role in aiding the brave few who fight to keep the world safer and more prosperous every day, as well as those who seek to dominate the world and become titans in the modern day world of business and entrepreneurialism.

About the Author

Brendan Scott Ecker is a dynamic and accomplished individual with a Bachelor's Degree in Criminal Justice. He has worked as a Sheriff's deputy and police officer and has leveraged his experience to succeed as an entrepreneur, author, screenwriter, investor, and podcast host. Ecker is also a former college athlete and has excelled in various sports, showcasing his versatile skills and remarkable abilities to succeed.

Ecker is the host of "The Brendan Ecker Influence" podcast, where he shares insights on entrepreneurship, business, finance, law enforcement, world events, politics, and personal development. He is an accomplished entrepreneur, writer, and investor. Ecker's success has been attributed to his analytical, dynamic, and driven mindset. He is also known for his many achievements in High School sports, where he has won numerous awards and accolades in football, baseball, powerlifting, tennis, soccer, cross country, track, and basketball.

Author's Note

First things first - despite the attractive and slightly click-baited title I chose to use, this book is not only about becoming a police officer. This book is about becoming a police officer and so much more. This book is to teach and guide future police officers on how to get accepted into the police academy, graduate from the police academy, earn the badge, and how to keep the badge. This book is to assist future police officers in their journey of one day getting hired at a department they love, but also a guide to how to succeed in anything you genuinely want badly enough in life.

For many of the pictures I used in this book, I have blurred out the faces of those within them, as many of the individuals have either not been asked to be in this book or are still active-duty police officers today. To conceal their identities, I felt it necessary to respect their privacy and keep their faces or visible last names hidden. This is for their own safety and common courtesy.

This book is an integration of both my experiences as a rookie cop and an entrepreneur. You will be able to analyze my successes and failures and use them to your advantage on your path to becoming a police officer, entrepreneur, or whatever it is that makes you truly passionate.

This book will change your perspective on everything society has taught you growing up, and it will make you open your mind to a different point of view. You won't think the way your parents may have taught you to think after reading this book. You will get more than just an education into what Law Enforcement is and was for me. This book was written to give honest details about the everyday life of a police officer and what it takes to turn the dream of becoming one into a reality. It is also about expanding your horizons and considering all options in life besides a life of solely dedicating every waking second to Law Enforcement once you are finally hired, and perhaps, maybe looking for something more in life. In that case, this book will be a great resource for you.

In this book, you will be learning immensely important information that will undoubtedly reconstruct and improve your perception of the world and your visions for the future. I will teach you to think big, to become mysteriously tenacious while simultaneously conquering everything in your path so that you can enjoy the life that you haven't even come to imagine yet. I will teach you to be confident and ruthlessly focused on success in all endeavors.

The truth is, Success comes to those who create their own opportunities. You must be intentional. Success does not come to those who wait. That is a lie. That is precisely why the overwhelming majority struggle and fail. You can't be weak, and you can't be lazy. If you haven't noticed, most people are just that. Every decision is critical, and every movement is vital. Many are not self-aware and are completely oblivious to what is happening around them. Weakness and carelessness will destroy you in today's competitive arena. If you are strong, prudent, industrious, motivated, fearless, humble, discerning, and unshakeable - then you will find Success in all endeavors. You will be a great police officer and, most importantly, a finer husband and father or wife and mother. If any person disagrees, respectfully decline and proceed to fulfill a purpose. They will only continue to sink while you swim. While others never learn about the ark and drown, you will get on the ark, and you will survive.

It is that exact mindset that this book will give you exposure to. I will change your mindset, rewire your way of thinking, and teach you how to become a police officer and a highly effective individual in all aspects of life. I will talk about what I remember being some of the most important lessons in my journey along the way and how I essentially failed my way to success as a police officer, writer, and entrepreneur.

Being a police officer is kind of like being a U.F.C. fighter. Both a U.F.C. fighter and a police officer get beat up regularly; they're terribly financially illiterate, they push themselves to extremely high standards, and they both have a reputation for being "cool," "badass," or "unique" in their respective professions. But the biggest similarity of all, sadly, is that both careers often leave extreme damage and trauma to the U.F.C. fighter and the police officer, especially if they are not careful with every punch, kick, block, or traffic stop in that sense. This book is a playbook on how to avoid the trauma of the traffic stops we all make in life. What you're reading is a Bible on how to achieve triumph in not just the career of Law Enforcement - but, most importantly, everyday life. By the end of this book, you will be ready to become a police officer and anything else you want to become. I will show you the keys to your American Dream.

My goal is to teach you how to avoid the trials and errors that I endured in my journey to becoming a police officer, how to get out of the career alive, and how to get out of it financially free. I am not a financial advisor, but I am an investor, entrepreneur, writer, as well as a police officer, and I know how to think big and execute bigger. I've spent countless hours studying the habits of billionaires, successful police officers, entrepreneurs, and highly effective people. This book will reveal the many hidden secrets to achieving any goal and becoming the best in whatever industry it is you select as your chosen niche.

Being in a job that you risk your life in comes with the importance of securing a fallback plan and at least seven streams of income at a minimum. This way, if you ever did fail to become a police officer, you would have other motivations, aspirations, focal points, and passions, and you could rest assured knowing that the world is filled with limitless possibilities and opportunities. No setback is anything short of a setup. How you choose to use it relies only upon you. There is plenty of achievement and wealth to go around - you just have to find it and attack it like a lion attacking a gazelle. You have to have a killer's mindset, an intention to swim the sharks, and a standard to only run with the beasts. You must be an unstoppable force, like a monster in the night that the world is afraid to battle. Your skin must be thick, your body ready for war, and your mind a fortress of solitude and unlimited strength. Then, you must channel it, control the power, and use it for the good of humanity and, of course, your own Legacy.

In this book, I will do my absolute best to remain politically neutral, accurate in my testimony, and strong in my convictions. I want to do everything I can to help you understand what life in Law Enforcement entails, how to become a police officer, a leader rather than a follower, and how to become everything that you seek to become. I wrote this self-help autobiography to provide some helpful options in terms of how to maneuver through the obstacles that you will likely face when pursuing a career as a police officer or as any kind of successful player in the game of money and life.

Introduction

If you are reading this, then you are seeking to become more in life, to help people, and hopefully become a police officer in this journey. I commend you for it, and I wish you luck in your endeavors, especially in today's political and social climate. I loved being a police officer. It was truly worth the hard work and many, many setbacks.

Without Law Enforcement, I would have never been able to help the people I have, I would have never been able to start my companies, and I would have never been able to build a life of prosperity and financial freedom for myself. I would have never seen the things I have, and I would have never met the people I did, which is the most important part of the job. I had a great first career that provided me with a solid paycheck and good benefits. It allowed me to save my money and later start my business.

Today, because of the hard work and hard times that I pushed through, and because of the time I served as a police officer, I learned how to be wealthy, and I matured from boyhood to manhood. I learned to play the game of life (no, not the board game. I'm talking about real life). This book will tell you how I learned to win that game.

I am fulfilling the final chapter's goal of this book, which is to pay it forward and to teach the next line of warriors everything that I learned as a police officer so that one day, you may be able to do the same. The goal is to educate future law enforcement officers and young entrepreneurs and to inspire motivated individuals to chase their dreams and join the fraternity of Law Enforcement. The road to success will not be easy in becoming a police officer or becoming anything you truly want to be in life. At the end of the day, with a little bit of luck and some broken pride… you might just make it out alive.

In this book, you will learn how to become a police officer and what it takes to accomplish such a goal. You will learn about some of my own experiences in Law Enforcement as a police officer fresh out of the academy and from when I was just a High School athlete doing ride-alongs with the Detroit City Police Department. I will talk about many of my own experiences and mistakes made so that you can learn from them in this book and, hopefully avoid the hurdles I had to overcome. This book is not just a book that will teach you how to become a police officer, but it is also a helpful guide if you are looking to earn that promotion, become a better employee, parent, or spouse, or just become a better person in general.

You will learn a lot about Law Enforcement that you didn't know before, and you will also learn how to keep your job after you've finally become a police officer. A lot of the valuable information and advice I will be providing comes directly from my own mistakes made along the way of developing my Law Enforcement resume and background, as well as mistakes made by other officers I have worked alongside. There is a plethora of information and experience that will most certainly help you in your journey to soon becoming a police officer. This book will assist in further understanding the Criminal Justice system in America and what it's really like to be a Law Enforcement Officer from my own training, education, and experience as a young, Middle Class, 23-year-old cop and entrepreneur from Eastern Michigan.

Before we get more into who I am, one should know what a police officer is first, as today's generation has a lack of understanding in terms of what the life of a police officer actually entails. You should know whether or not this career is for you and whether or not you even have the prerequisites to pursue this career to begin with. Unfortunately, not everyone can become a police officer. It isn't because they wouldn't be great ones, but rather because there is simply a base set of requirements that have to be met. There are certain standards that are expected to be reached. There are many steps involved in becoming a police officer. There are many exams to pass and many ways to find yourself disqualified for even the most minor reasons.

The entire process just to get accepted into the police academy (nonetheless graduate and hopefully get hired) is brutally difficult, long, strenuous, backbreaking, nerve-racking, tedious, physically and mentally exhausting, all the while immensely character-building. It is one of my more difficult accomplishments out of my many accomplishments in life, if not the most difficult. That is simply the truth. However, it is absolutely achievable, and I highly implore you to pursue this journey of pure adversity and extraordinary reward if you are interested in saving lives and making a difference.

Becoming a police officer means that you have no more social life. No more social media, no more parties, and no more getting yourself into trouble. You have to be okay with being private, isolated, and boring outside of your work life if you plan on becoming a police officer and keeping your job. Some officers would disagree and say, "You have to have fun in this job," which is obviously true, but you also have to be very careful, and you should remain on the down low when it comes to your personal/social life. Everything becomes about family, finances, the brothers and sisters in your department, and the future of your career once you settle into the lifestyle of a full-time police officer. You are now simple on paper, an employee, a member of the Middle Class, and also feared by the public due to your position of influence and power. In real-time, you're driving lights and sirens, rushing to a home invasion or P.I.A (Personal Injury Accident), and getting paid by the hour.

In this book, I'm going to tell you all about how to become a police officer, what to expect in the basic police academy, and how to succeed in your first Law Enforcement job. The reason I wrote this book is because I remember what it was like going through the police academy and getting hired at my first Sheriff's Department. I remember there being very little information on what it was actually like, and what I was to expect. There wasn't much information available on Google that answered my many questions about what to expect in the police academy and in the profession itself. I wanted to write this to help guide and motivate ambitious leaders who seek to one day wear the badge and serve their communities.

I want to inform people about some things the internet will never tell you about a career in Law Enforcement. I want people to be prepared for what the job will bring, and I want them to walk into the career with the extra advantage of knowing the important things that I didn't when I was first coming onto the force. This is why I wrote this book.

When I first started out as a cop after being hired at the department of my dreams, I felt as if I was thrown into service and expected to know everything. My F.T.Os (Field Training Officers) expected me to know the job inside and out as if I had been a cop for ten years already when I was just a rookie with little to no real experience and fresh out of the academy. I didn't know anything about how to do the job. Even though I had a Bachelor's Degree in Criminal Justice at the time, the fact is, college never taught me much, and the Police Academy only teaches you the bare minimum. I remember feeling completely lost and misguided when I started at my first department. My F.T.Os acted as if they were actually teaching me and insisted that they were giving me a chance after chance. This was not the case. So many of my F.T.Os would tell me, "Never be afraid to ask questions. It's good to ask questions." So, of course, I would ask my F.T.Os questions. But I hardly ever got actual answers to the questions I would ask.

I would ask my question, and my F.T.Os would respond with remarks like "You should already know that" or "What do you think the answer is"? I'm not kidding. This really happened, and it happened a lot! I would ask my F.T.O. a question, and they would answer my questions with more questions that I didn't know. They would make me second guess myself, and I would forget what I had even asked to begin with. Then, moments later, they would look at me like I was an idiot when I screwed up because I didn't know the answer, to begin with, and never got any real answers. Needless to say, I would never end up learning anything, and I would never get simple answers to simple questions.

I had to learn this job myself, for the most part, with virtually zero guidance from people who thought they were giving me good guidance. The only real thing I did learn during my F.T.O program at that first department was that you shouldn't ask questions; you seek answers. If you don't know something, figure it out on your own, or lose your job. I guess, in some ways, I learned something from the first police department I worked for. I thought that the same department was my dream department when in reality, it was actually a living nightmare.

Ultimately, as you can guess, I was often left without my questions answered, and it led to me having to resign from that agency. I was thrown into the job and expected to know it all. If I would have had a book like this, I would have been a lot more prepared than I was, and I would have avoided a lot of mistakes. I had to learn this job on my own in many ways, despite the different F.T.O. programs I've done. The department I worked for next paid me better and treated me better. So, in the end, no harm was done, and I ended up exactly where I needed to be.

If you learn from my successes and failures that I will discuss in this book, you will be ready for everything the police academy will throw at you, and you will be exceptionally more prepared for when you eventually get hired into a department. If you take the time to read or listen to this book all the way through, then you will find yourself joining those who represent the thin blue line and America's finest defenders of Law and Order. If you simply listen and if you simply apply the knowledge I provide in this guide to becoming a police officer, then you will succeed, and you will become an agent of Law Enforcement and more than you ever thought imaginable before deciding to read this book.

There is only one rule that I have for you - Do. Not. Quit. You must keep going - always. The journey to becoming a police officer or anything in life is not easy. You may very well stumble and struggle. If I chose to quit after having failed the state licensing exam, after already graduating from that first police academy, I would have never become a police officer today, and you would never be reading this book.

Nothing you do in life will ever be easy. You have to earn it and take what you want. Becoming a police officer, it is the same. The journey to be a police officer will be mentally, physically, spiritually, and socially demanding. It will challenge you, and it will push you to your limits. But remember - if something doesn't challenge you, then it will never change you. If you want it bad enough, then you must continue to pursue this dream no matter how difficult the road may be. If you simply stay focused and never quit, then you will find yourself successful on the other side - and finally satisfied with your results. If I managed to accomplish all of it, then you can manage to accomplish all of it. If you follow this one rule and never quit, you will achieve your goal, and you will become a police officer. That, I guarantee.

Unfortunately, it is challenging to become a police officer, and for that reason, I want to respect your time and advise you of some of the reasons candidates may not ever become police officers. Time is the most valuable asset, and I want to respect yours. In doing this, you can learn whether or not this career is for you early and begin chasing a different career that may be better suited for you. Before you decide to enter this profession, you should know what a police officer is, what the job entails, and what the job will demand of you. I will explain the profession and hopefully answer any questions you may have.

In reading this book, you will learn the philosophy and psychology of a police officer, and you will learn about the everyday life of a police officer. It is rewarding to be one who stands on the thin blue line between the forces of good and evil. It pays to take risks, to dare, to dream, but most importantly, to take action and to succeed in your desired journey. In many ways, you must be willing to put yourself in the arena of life if you seek Greatness and Triumph. If you want to be a police officer, the journey is hard and far from easy. But if you are disciplined, qualified by merit and good life choices, willing to simply try, and never quit, then you will earn the badge and find yourself dining at the table of warriors and defenders. Don't be afraid to put yourself in the arena. As Theodore Roosevelt once said;

"It is not the critic who counts, not the man who points out how the strong man stumbles or where the doer of deeds could have done them better. The credit belongs to the man who is actually in the arena, whose face is marred

by dust and sweat and blood; who strives valiantly; who errs, who comes short again and again, because there is no effort without error and shortcoming; but who does actually strive to do the deeds; who knows great enthusiasms, the great devotions; who spends himself in a worthy cause; who at best knows, in the end, the triumph of high achievement, and who at the worst, if he fails, at least fails while daring greatly, so that his place shall never be with those cold and timid souls who neither knows victory nor defeat."

PART I: Education, Research, and the Decision (The Easy Part)

Chapter 1: What is a Police Officer? What Does It Take to Become One?

The first police department in the United States was established in New York City in 1844 (it was officially organized in 1845), but much of the current law enforcement philosophy is still heavily based on Sir Robert Peel's ideals and principles. Peele was a British Conservative statesman who was Prime Minister of the United Kingdom twice while also serving as Chancellor of the Exchequer and Home Secretary. Robert Peele is widely regarded as the "Father of Modern Policing."

Rober Peel's revered commissioners established a set of policing principles and values that are just as important and critical today as they were two centuries ago, and it is because of this that other prominent figures, such as August Vollmer, were able to carry on the torch as some of the first founders of Law Enforcement.

August Vollmer was a forward-thinking police chief who made Berkeley the epicenter of his innovations. In the early 1900s, he became Berkeley's first police chief and began to advance policing through the use of technology, training, and, most importantly, education. August Vollmer established the first centralized police records system, which was designed to streamline and organize criminal investigations. He set up a call box network. He also taught his deputies how to shoot. Vollmer's reputation as the "Father of Modern Law Enforcement" grew over time.

What many don't know is that the full acronym of "P.O.L.I.C.E" stands for "Public Officer for Legal Investigations and Criminal Emergencies." We are typically Type A individuals. We are both warriors and guardians responsible for ensuring that law and order remain intact. We are a group of personnel who are there to enforce laws, prevent any kind of civil disorder, save lives if needed, and maintain the laws which stand against criminal activity accordingly and justly.

Police officers are average men and women who have been trained and entrusted to respond to emergency situations and to protect the innocent in their communities. They have been paid for by the American taxpayer to enforce the laws of the Constitution in good faith, with the intent of maintaining and protecting the fundamental Rights and Freedoms granted to society by our Creator. That is essentially the role of a police officer in society. If you are considering getting into this career, you should already know whether or not you want to take risks, make sacrifices, and uphold the responsibilities that come with the job. If not, as stated before, there are other great career fields out there that pay far more money and far less risk.

You will never become a multimillionaire by being a cop anyways, so if you can't become one for some reason, then so what! Now you can rest easy knowing that you still have a chance to make good money and to do something that doesn't potentially result in your death. At the end of the day, you can always become an entrepreneur, make a few good investments, and start your own business. In that case, you'd be doing so well that you'd probably be buying my entire department.

It takes a different breed to volunteer for high-risk and low-pay. It takes a lot of drive and commitment on top of that. I want people going into Law Enforcement to know the truth. I want people to know what they are getting into. Being a police officer indeed makes one powerful, but it is also a heavy responsibility. Being a police officer is simply not an easy job. It requires a sturdy soul and thick skin. You will work on holidays and weekends, and you will work when you are exhausted. You will work your 8, 10, or 12-hour shift when you are injured and when the family life is out of balance. You are always working, and it feels that way. The days often drag on, and you will be mentally exhausted by the end of each shift because you will have already handled 12 C.F.S '(Calls for Service) within one 12-hour shift. You will be tired and uncomfortable often, and you will be mentally drained and feel like you're on autopilot every day. The solution to this is simple… Get comfortable with being tired and uncomfortable.

You will be spat upon, disrespected, insulted, and assaulted, and you will pay the price for the power you will be privileged to withhold as a police officer, especially depending on where you are a police officer at. You will pay the price of danger and risk for the privilege of power granted to you by the state and God himself. You are enforcing the laws of the United States government - the most powerful government in the world. You have the ability to take a person's Constitutional rights away. Simply by being entrusted with the ultimate decision to arrest or not arrest - is power. As stated by Ben Parker in Spider-Man, "With great power comes great responsibility."

Chapter 2: Why I Became a Police Officer

I always knew I was going to end up becoming a police officer or something related to it. As a young kid from around 4-12 years old, I wanted to be a professional baseball player. Obviously, as time went on, I realized that wasn't going to happen. Not only that but also, I began to want something more in life. I started to feel like my purpose was for something greater.

At around 13 years old, I then developed an obsession with the Marine Corps. I watched movies like "Jarhead," "Full Metal Jacket," and "The Marine," starring John Cena (one of my favorite wrestlers). I even kept a log of how far I would run every single day until I felt like I was ready to go through Paris Island boot camp and survive. I was already very athletic and in pretty good shape, but I wanted to have an Eight-pack, I wanted to look ripped, and I wanted to be ready for the day when I got off that bus in San Diego for boot camp. I found myself eventually getting that eight-pack, looking as perfect as I could to my own standards, but then… my ambitions grew even larger, and I needed more.

As time went on, right around when 7th grade began, I started to expand my horizons. I remember seeing the movies like "300", "Act of Valor," and "Navy Seals" and knew I had to get even better than I was, and I needed to get even stronger if I ever wanted to be the best of the best in the warrior class. If I wanted to dine at the table of warriors, I would have to push myself to the limits even more. I started taking freezing showers so I could train my mind and body to accept extreme pain and discomfort. When I was in track, I remember sprinting the entire 1600 meters (1 Mile) in 5:40 seconds (my fastest mile ever completed). I only accomplished this because of how badly I wanted to be ready for BUD/s and become a Navy Seal.

Being a Navy Seal is a dream I had for many years, all the way up to my Junior year in High School, and I was very dedicated to it. I believed that I was going to be a Navy Seal after I graduated, and I was serious about it. I put in the work and built my strength through football and powerlifting, along with many other sports I played. I went to recruiting offices and did whatever I could to accomplish my goal of getting on the fast track to BUD/s. This journey led to my career in Law Enforcement after graduating from college. I remember watching "Welcome to Buds Class 234" on YouTube and thinking, "I have to do that."

Sports were a big part of how I became a police officer, mainly because I used sports to train me for the military (what I thought my career would be). Cross Country was my way of preparing for the grueling 4-mile distance runs I would have to do in BUDs (Basic Underwater Demolition), which is Seal Training. I started off as an out-of-shape kid with asthma but later found myself placing top 10 in every single cross-country race I participated in. All because I knew that in BUD/s, to my knowledge, you had to run 4 miles in 28 minutes. So cross country was my own way of training me for that.

Football was a way of training my body to endure pain and to win in hand-to-hand combat no matter how tired, sore, or defeated I felt. I didn't get voted Defensive M.V.P. by my High School football team by accident. They voted for me because I cared about them, and I put them first on the field. I care about my brothers. I put the squad first always, and by doing this, I was able to later play in college and eventually become a police officer.

I cared about my brothers on the field just like I would care about my fellow warriors in the field of combat. Just like I would take a bullet for any fellow officer in a heartbeat if it meant getting them back home safely to their families, that was my perspective on football, and it's how I felt in regard to attaining my goal of becoming a Navy Seal. Football is a great teacher and a great builder of character. Football maketh a man.

Baseball taught me the values of brotherhood. I played baseball longer than any other sport. I've played soccer, basketball, and tennis, and spent some time in track, football, powerlifting... pretty much everything... but baseball was the first sport I ever played and the sport I played all the way up until my sophomore year in college, along with football. Baseball taught me a lot about patience, sportsmanship, maintaining composure, and leadership. Especially composure, considering that striking out or making an error can completely destroy your game if you lose your head and don't know how to shake it off.

In baseball, just like in life, you have to shake it off and keep your cool when you strike out or make an error. You have to get ready for the next play or the next at-bat and forget about the past. Your team is counting on you to perform and represent. This is what I mean when I say that baseball taught me patience, as it was more mentally demanding than any sport I've played out of the many I've played. Although football was also mentally demanding, it was more of a contact sport and physical. Baseball was a mental game to me, while football was more physically based. In football, as long as you know your route, put 100% into every play, and remember your playbook - then you will do just fine. In baseball, no matter how hard you try, no matter how much you know the game, if you can't relax and focus, then you will make errors, and you will strike out every time. Tennis was very much the same in my experience. In tennis, just like baseball, it was a very mentally demanding sport. Like baseball, you can know the game and give your 100% effort, but if you don't relax your mind and focus, then you will make numerous mistakes and find yourself losing every match, every set.

I was on a travel baseball team, and it was the same roster for seven years. We played together up until we were all about 16, when we finally disbanded the squad and went our separate ways. However, we were a unit throughout those seven years playing together. We were a clique. We were a family. We were brothers - just like a Seal team, and that's how I always thought of it. If another team messed with any of us, we were all at war with that other team. Today, I think very similarly about my fellow police officers. We are the few who stand on the thin line between good and evil and risk EVERYTHING for it, with very little reward in exchange for that risk.

Baseball taught me that you can't give up after a few strikeouts or errors. In life, it all comes down to making fewer mistakes than the other team and simply making one big play - and, most importantly, knowing how to do it under pressure. How will you perform under pressure when the bases are loaded and the game is tied with two outs and two strikes against you? Life is a lot like that. Learning how to perform under pressure when it matters most. These decisions lead to success or failure, whether we like it or not.

Being a police officer comes down to making fewer mistakes than the dangerous people we often deal with. It comes down to one big decision and being able to make the right one under extreme pressure. Most cannot handle the pressure, and they get crushed in the world. Being a cop or an entrepreneur requires one to know how to do it under pressure, when people are recording you, shouting at you, testing you, and depending on you. Knowing when to use or not to use deadly force, or knowing when to continue or terminate a pursuit, for example, are small examples of being able to perform under pressure in the job of Law Enforcement. Baseball taught me how to perform under pressure.

When I was in Middle School, I would swim at the rec center and conduct similar swim evolutions I watched in the "BUD/s Class 234: It Pays to be a Winner" documentary. I would do the dolphin swim, submerged 25-meter swims, tread water for an hour, and see how long I could stay at the bottom of that 15-foot pool. I did anything I could to simulate what BUD/s would be like. Every time I accomplished a goal, I would imagine myself doing inspections in boot camp and the instructors saying, "Not good enough. Do it again and do it better", so I would do it again, and I would do it better - again, and again, and again until I felt I was ready for Seal training.

I built a mentality that anything and everything could always be made better and improved upon. Today, I can't reverse this mindset. It is second nature to push myself to my limits and be the best that I can possibly be. This eventually helped me in becoming a police officer because doing things right and having high standards for myself allowed me to make good decisions and keep a proper balance on everything else in my life. Equilibrium is everything.

I always imagined myself in the flats of Coronado, California, or the mucks of Virginia Beach, Virginia. I wanted to be a U.D.T Seal diver more than anything, and this dream eventually led me to my career in Law Enforcement. I wanted to be blacked out in scuba gear using the sonar draggers and conducting H.A.L.O jumps with an M4A1 Carbine and German Shepherd attached to my chest. I wanted that life. I was inspired by Mark Owen's book, "No Easy Day," which was an autobiography of how Seal Team Six (DEVGRU) assassinated Osama Bin Laden on May 2nd, 2011. For those who are unaware, Osama Bin Laden was a former CIA analyst and the suspected mastermind of the 9/11 hijacking and World Trade Center bombings. I highly recommend reading Mark Owen's book, as it is a fantastic insight into the life of the U.S military and Naval Special Warfare Operations. We all owe a debt to the brave warriors of our armed forces, especially the damn few who risk their lives every day for our Freedom.

Moral of the story - sports were a way of training my mind and my body for one day climbing the ladder so I could become a Special Forces operator. I was hooked on the idea of going to dangerous places nobody would ever dare go, and I relished the concept of working in a clique of elite fighters that were just as motivated and focused as me to accomplish a seemingly impossible objective. I wanted to take out the most dangerous terrorists like Osama Bin Laden and be the rock that chaos and anarchy broke against - but none of that ended up happening until I graduated from college and became a cop. For me, there was another path that made more sense, and this was the path I stuck to. Law Enforcement allowed me to remain on this path, just by a different function.

Fast forward to my senior year of high school. I then woke up one day and realized that being a police officer would be a lot more sustainable and sensible. I still wanted to see my family and have a normal life, and my visions had changed. Mainly, this was due to the recruiters in our school spamming me and never leaving me alone. Strangely enough, it was the recruiters who pushed me into the path of Law Enforcement and away from the path of the military. When the recruiters learned that I was interested in working my way to BUDs in the hopes of becoming a Seal, and once they had learned that I was a tri-athlete in my High School, they began spamming my phones, and they never left me alone. In all honesty, it got annoying, and it pushed me away from my dream of becoming a Seal. But this wasn't the only reason I abandoned my dreams of becoming a Seal.

Having to leave my family for over 265 days plus a year was another reason I didn't want to continue the road to Special Warfare operations. I had also begun to realize that we needed brave souls on American soil defending the innocent, not just overseas. I was already in a public safety class at my vocational school for a few years of training for this, and I had already conducted two ride-alongs with Detroit City Police Department by the time I was accepted to Olivet College to play football and baseball. I had already built strong connections and experiences through combines, college visits, and showcase tournaments. It was then decided that Law Enforcement would be my chosen profession.

After making the decision to become a police officer, I dedicated and immersed myself in the career fully. I found myself in a position to choose whichever college I wanted to go to so I could not only play football and baseball still but also get an education in Criminal Justice.

I found myself going to 13 different college visits and several showcases combined for baseball and football. I was serious about getting that degree, regardless of how much it cost - so needless to say, I was set on success in finding a place to both play sports and hone my craft. Part of me still wanted to accomplish that challenge of getting a degree, and I wanted to be able to say that I got my degree. Despite the student loan debt I had to overcome, I'm proud to have that little piece of worthless paper proving I have a Bachelor's Degree in Criminal Justice - because it helped me get accepted into the police academy, which later helped me write this book and start my other business ventures.

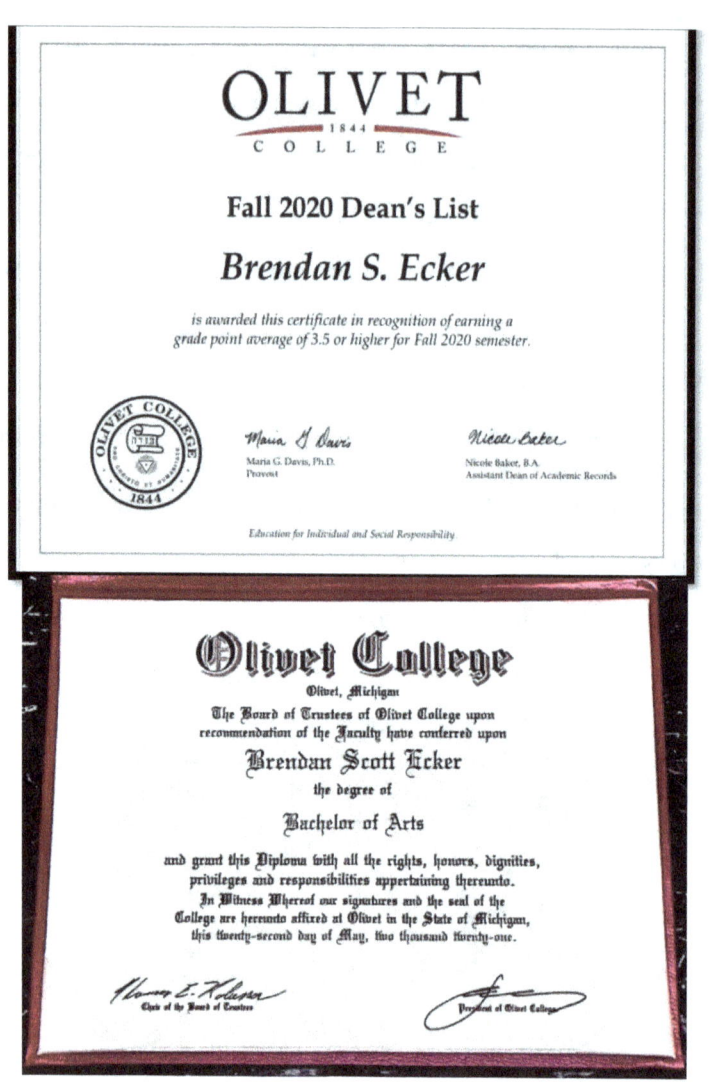

Another reason I am proud of the degree I obtained is that the credentials of having a degree are good to have, and it displays your ability to be consistent, persistent, and patient. Once you have a degree, no one can ever take it away from you. You always have something to fall back on. Although many degrees in today's society are worthless, it says a lot about any individual who has the patience and commitment to endure and overcome the liberally dominated societies we call "College Universities." This was not easy for me, as I have always been a strong conservative for the most part. Fortunately, I was socially liberal and fiscally conservative overall, so I was able to survive just enough to earn the degree.

I remember my favorite colleges being the private colleges and a few of the public universities. I remember that my favorite schools were, of course, Olivet College (where I eventually graduated), but also Tiffin University in Ohio, Grand Valley University, Saginaw Valley University, Northern Michigan University, Western Michigan University, Alma College, Albion College, Carthage College in Wisconsin, and Trine University in Indiana. In the end, it came down to Olivet, Trine, Tiffin, Alma, and Saginaw Valley. Olivet offered me a full ride, and the others didn't, so of course, I had to choose Olivet.

From then on, I cleaned up my act and stopped getting into trouble with my friends. I stopped doing stupid stuff in school just to get a laugh and popularity. I started making better choices and took my grades more seriously. I focused on academics right alongside football, powerlifting, and baseball. I put my long-term goals and my future ahead of my short-term gains and my past. I started going on college visits and combines so I could get into college. I did everything I could to boost my GPA up. I shook as many hands as I could so I could get on a college football roster. At that point, Law Enforcement became my new goal, and it is a goal I pursued throughout college up to the time I decided to write this book. It is a goal that I accomplished, and it is a goal that I now am hoping to teach you how to accomplish.

Chapter 3: How Badly Do You Want It?

Before you even consider applying for a local police academy, you should ask yourself how badly you want to be a police officer. The following questions should be asked. These are all common reasons why people constantly get washed out of the police academy because they didn't ask themselves these questions soon enough:

1. Am I U.S Citizen?
2. Am I 18 years old?
3. Have I ever been convicted of a Misdemeanor or Felony? If so, can I explain it and defend it?
4. How are my driving record and driving status? Am I valid? Do I have any points?
5. Do I have any warrants out for my arrest?
6. Do I have an updated Driver's License, Insurance, and Registration?
7. Do I have a High School diploma?
8. Do I have at least an Associate's Degree?
9. Do I have a Bachelor's degree or higher?
10. Have I ever been suspended from school? If so, what for?
11. Have I ever been sued?
12. Could I pass a drug test today if I was given one?
13. Do I have good vision?

14. Am I color blind?
15. Do I lack depth perception?
16. Am I hard of hearing?
17. Do I have a speech impediment?
18. Do I have any medical disorders? If so, will they disqualify me?
19. Have I ever suffered a traumatic brain injury or any injury that hinders my ability to drive currently?
20. Can I run a mile without stopping? How long can I sprint for?
21. Can I do at least 20-40 pushups in 60 seconds?
22. Can I do at least 30-40 situps in 60 seconds?
23. Do I have a good enough vertical jump for police academy standards?
24. Could I pass a psychological evaluation? How do you score on the Meyers Briggs Personality Test and the MMPI test (what you will most likely be tested on)
25. Could I pass a background check?
26. Could I pass a polygraph exam?
27. Do I have a social media that is clean and professional (no politics, cursing, racism, or discrimination)?

28. Do I have a clean house for when the police department of my dreams wants to do a home interview with me?
29. Am I willing to be shot at if hired for duty?
30. Would I shoot back if I was shot at?
31. Am I willing to make low pay for high risk?
32. What do I have to lose? Am I willing to sacrifice it?
33. Can I truly say, without question, that I was born to be a police officer?

If you are considering the career of a police officer, you should ask yourselves the questions listed above. If you can't definitively answer them, then I would start reconsidering and making sure that Law Enforcement is the career that will truly make you the happiest. I would evaluate all of the questions I left for you, and if everything checks clear, then continue pursuing this path. If not, there are other careers out there. There is no shame in getting paid a lot more money for doing something else with a lot less risk - in fact, in many ways, the smarter person would choose that route. Unless you've got a hero's mentality and a warrior's mindset, and unless you're willing to be a slave to the government and to the community you serve who pays your taxes, there is nothing wrong with taking another path and living a much less stressful life.

You have to change a few things about yourself if you do not match the profile I described in the paragraph above. Even I had to change drastically when it came to many of those issues. I had gotten in big trouble for such things in multiple instances, both when I was in the police academy and hired at my first department. I can't stress it enough - you have to be careful and cautious… you have to be very covert about who you are, what you do, and where you work. Any of my academy instructors or former Sergeants would be willing to tell you the same thing. I will discuss how I learned those lessons in the chapters ahead.

Another fact you should know before considering this profession is that Law Enforcement is not what the media or Hollywood makes it out to be. The overwhelming majority of police officers that I have met and worked with are very upstanding, good people. The media tries its hardest to paint a picture that all police are racists, criminals, tyrants, incompetent, and corrupt. None of this is true from my experience as a police officer. In fact, it is quite the opposite, and quite often, those same politicians who accuse the police of such things are quite often far more racist, criminal, tyrannical, incompetent, or corrupt than anyone you will meet working in the circles of Law Enforcement.

I mean, when you think about it, we, as the police, are members of the Executive Branch. We can only enforce the laws that have already been passed and signed into law.

Politicians are in the Legislative Branch, which means that they are the ones who create and vote on the bills and, ultimately, decide which bills become laws. So in that logic, who do you think has more power over such the social issues I have mentioned? Police Officers or Politicians? I will blame the politicians before I blame the police. We aren't superheroes, and we don't get away with breaking the law, but we do see a lot on the job that television could never, should never, and would never show people.

We are regular human beings who worked our asses off, made just enough correct decisions in life to make it on the government side of the spectrum, and, quite honestly, are just normal people who managed to get a license to fight crime and serve a cause. We all still put our pants on one leg at a time, just like anyone else. We have the same problems with health, family, friends, and finances that everyone else does. Nothing is much different in the everyday life of a cop. The attention and respect you get from people are about the only thing that changes when you have the uniform on. Not to mention the pressure of being able to do your job when called upon. You always have to perform. Fucking up at work leads to getting fired or, God forbid, your own funeral. Otherwise, cops are just like everyone else. We have to abide by the same laws, and we can't enforce unlawful ones. Plain and simple. Close and shut.

Every officer is a little different. I've known cops who were excellent at their jobs and aggressive in catching criminals, some who were careless and lazy, some who were calmer and laid back, and some who were selfish and downright rude to everyone they spoke to. Every officer has a different personality, but in general, most are ordinary and good-intentioned people. The police officers I've come to work with and know were all usually very exceptional, driven, focused, confident, intelligent, competitive, and even more than anything else... very, very, very, very cocky. Despite this, every police officer I have come to know has proven to be a brave, tough, wise, and fearless leader. Police Officers are not how the media portray them to be whatsoever.

We are trained to know and enforce the laws endowed by our Founding Fathers. People should know that being a police officer is really just another job... but also a dangerous job. You should be ready for the day when you may have to draw your firearm. You should be ready for the day when you may have to engage in deadly force and shoot back at someone who is shooting at you. I am lucky enough that I have never been in a firefight, but if I did ever have to fire back one day, I like to believe that I would be ready and that I would act swiftly for the safety of myself, my partner, and those around me. I hope that I will never have to use my firearm, but I will be ready, and I will use it if I absolutely have to in order to defend the innocent and myself. Every waking day being a cop could be your last if you are not careful with a sense of urgency. Remember that you are risking your life being a police officer. It is not a job where you sit at a desk and crunch numbers to make someone else rich. You may have to pull your firearm - so be ready to act if called upon.

You should be able to say the same, and you should get excited when you think about the chance to save a life. You should get excited when you think about making that perfect traffic stop. You should get excited thinking about getting drunk drivers off the road. You should get excited when you think about putting on the uniform every day. You should get excited when you think about getting to drive a police cruiser. Get excited to pack your first gear bag. You might just stumble across a good chunk of cocaine on the basic pretext traffic stop and make the biggest arrest of your life. You should get excited about possibly having to deliver a newborn baby on duty one day. You should get excited about arresting sex offenders, and child abusers, de-escalating domestic violence situations, and stopping career criminals. This is a fun job and rewarding job if done correctly and with passion. Being a police officer is one of the greatest careers in the world if you truly want it badly enough and if you enjoy the sacrifice and adrenaline. It is so much more than just a job. It is a passion, an adventure, a dream, a challenge, a privilege, and above all else - a calling. The real question should be whether or not it is your calling.

In reading this, it is my hope that you will become motivated enough to challenge yourself and get through the police academy. Today, America needs more cops and especially good cops. There has never been a higher number of police officers quitting their jobs due to greedy and corrupt politicians making officers 'lives a living Hell. Politicians and the mainstream media have fueled racial tensions across the planet, and Law Enforcement is continuously attacked since the George Floyd incident occurred in May of 2020. We need brave men and women who are strong enough to fight against evil and humble enough to endure a constantly changing environment and perception of Law Enforcement. Especially in the extremely volatile and sensitive society we live in today. We need cops who will take accountability, do the right thing, and make swift, prudent decisions under high-pressure situations.

I want the audience to know that I am willing to accept the negative image I may receive after publishing this book. It should be understood that this book was written to simply tell my story of events from when I was a police officer and how I got myself into and through the police academy. My opinions are based on my own experiences and observations of being both an entrepreneur and a police officer.

Chapter 4: Staying Out Of Trouble - Show Me Your Friends...

If you haven't already realized, becoming a police officer requires one to be merely perfect on paper. Your driving record and a criminal record can make or break a career in Law Enforcement, and oftentimes, the people you associate yourself with can become major influences on such records. The direction of your life is very much decided by whom you choose to surround yourself with. Staying out of trouble is important to accomplishing the goal of becoming a police officer because when you find yourself interviewing for a position in the police academy, some of the questions you will be asked will be:

- Why do you want to become a police officer?
- How long have you wanted to be a police officer?
- Have you ever been suspended?
- Have you ever smoked marijuana, cocaine, methamphetamine, or any other controlled substance?
- How often do you consume alcohol on a weekly basis?
- Have you ever been fired from a previous job?
- Have you ever been involved in a lawsuit?
- Have you ever committed a Misdemeanor?

- Have you ever been convicted of a Felony?
- How many speeding tickets have you had? Parking tickets?
- Do you have any active warrants out for your arrest?
- Have you ever been in a fight?
- Would you be okay with pulling the trigger if you were hired as a police officer?
- If we were to contact your former bosses or teachers, what would they say about you?

These are only a short list of questions you will most likely be asked, many of which I have already discussed earlier in this book. These questions will be asked to you in both an oral board interview to be admitted into the police academy and for your first police job. How comfortable are you with answering these questions? This is why it is important to live a good life and to stay out of trouble. Show me your friends, and I'll show you who you are. If you surround yourself with Kings, then you, too, will be a King. If you surround yourself with thieves, then you, too, will be a thief. If you surround yourself with common men, then you, too, will be common. If you surround yourself with beggars, then you, too, will become a beggar. Choose to be a King and to be Royal. Better to live a life of wisdom and ease than one that will keep you at your knees. Be royal, and take the road less traveled. In doing this, you will shine among your peers, and you will become the natural leader of the flock. You will become the sheepdog rather than the sheep. Always ready to battle the wolves, but always prepared to defend the sheep. You will outwit, outsmart, and out-compete your competitors. In the end, you will walk with the Kings and soar with the eagles. You will eventually go from the sheepdog to the shepherd who orchestrates the flock, the sheepdog, and the wolves.

Granted, I can't rightfully sit here and tell you that I was perfect in my journey of becoming a police officer. I've always enjoyed the adventure of breaking the rules to a necessary extent. Especially when I was in Middle School and High School. I was friends with everyone, and my teachers loved me. However, I was always rebellious, and I gave my teachers a run for their money. I like to believe that to this day, they see me as a comeback kid and success story, but at the very least, I was likely a pain in their ass (to put it bluntly). This is something I never dared tell my police academy instructors when they were interviewing me or the police departments I worked for. Today, I wish I had mentioned this side of myself because it made me unique compared to the common competitor who is plain, boring, normal, overly respectful, ass kissing, and playing by the rules only until they get what they want. That always drove me crazy about any job interview I would attend. Everyone was fake, and everyone pretended to be someone they weren't.

To find someone who is really, truly honest and actually interesting was always something rare in any job that I competed for - and I was always brilliant in my job interviews, and I almost always got the job. Why? Because I did everything I could to be interesting and different from the rest of the flock and also present myself as a clear asset to the job I would interview for. I still would be overly polite and mannerable, but I HATED it because it wasn't real. Nobody is as nice and polite as they appear in a job interview. Nobody.

Most people present themselves as employable, perfect, charming, compassionate, and kind individuals simply as a way to get the job, and once they do, they change after about a month of working at that job. I always hated that because I never changed after any of the job interviews I attended. I was always myself and did what I could to be open and respectful. However, even with this track record of successful interviews I nailed and got the jobs for, I wish I had been more open about myself and my rocky background because, at the end of the day, our background is what makes us interesting and unique. Like any reality TV show, the drama and distinguished personas of each character in the show are what make them attractive and entertaining to the world. Being different, spontaneous, controversial, and strange in the human experience is precisely what is most entertaining to the audience (a.k.a, your interviewers) - so never be afraid to be dramatic and open about who you are as a human being. Be bold enough to be yourself.

If I am being honest with you and myself, I was charismatic, motivated, cocky, and athletic, but very nerdy, troublemaker, and jock. I loved playing sports, working out, chasing girls, making connections, meeting new people, being the center of attention, being a leader, stirring the pot, pushing the limits, having fun, playing video games, making deals, and studying the world. I enjoyed the arts, rich history, science, finance, business, economics, athletics, English literature, psychographics, and human psychology. I have always been fascinated by these subjects, and each subject taught me something priceless in my journey to becoming a published author, entrepreneur, and police officer.

Stirring the pot taught me to be a creative and critical thinker. I learned to observe human nature and study the likes and dislikes of those around me, which ultimately allowed me the opportunities to stir the pot and create controversial debates, ideas, and habits - just so I could further study the fallout of those actions and learn more from how others would respond to varying forms of stimuli, comfort, and also discomfort.

Pushing the limits taught me to succeed in anything I tried because I learned never to quit until I accomplished my intended goal. I finish what I start, and I see an objective through until the bitter end. This was evident in the many sports I played, those being soccer, tennis, basketball, baseball, football, and powerlifting. You have to push the limits in anything you do because if you don't, you will be average and forgotten. Not only will you be average and forgotten in the history books, but you will also become stagnant, complacent, and content with mediocrity. When you push yourself to the limits of absolute collapse and exhaustion, endure the pain that comes with life, and learn from your mistakes along the way, but still to the point of controllable behavior and action, then you will find yourself surpassing all of your peers 1,000 times over.

Having fun taught me that life is all about fun and not all about stress, bills, and playing life by the rules. Fuck the rules. Life is all about breaking the rules. Those who follow the rules and never have fun lose in life every single time. Playing by the rules gets you nowhere if I'm being transparent with you. Yes. I know that sounds weird coming from a cop. But the truth is, you can't be a great cop unless you have explored the boundaries of society's "rules" in life. You have to be an explorer, a creator, and an adventurer. Rules are made to be broken by the brave. All great minds in history were, by definition, rule breakers.

I have broken my fair share of rules in order to succeed and get ahead in life, and I am unapologetic about it. Make no mistake, and this doesn't mean that I chose to cut corners. I still worked my ass off for my success, but I still believe that I became a great cop because I was never afraid to be adventurous and have fun in life. You have to experience the unknown and face it head-on. I never allowed the rules of life to stop me from achieving my goals, aspirations, relationship-building, or wild ambitions that seemed impossible. I welcomed the unknown and was always curious about what lingered outside of the "normal" boundaries and rules of life. I never allowed school, or any kind of prison-like structure, to change who I was or what I wanted to accomplish. Even throughout the academy, I refused to be like everyone else. I enjoyed being Brendan Scott Ecker - that funny, mysterious, rebellious, and self-reliant guy. I have always been independent, driven, and wise enough to know right from wrong, so I didn't need anyone else to tell me how it was done. I was brave enough to make mistakes and learn from the mistakes because, from a young age, I always knew - that mistakes are what make us who we are.

Unfortunately, schools in today's era have become highly restrictive and punishing rather than fun and rewarding. I remember feeling like I was in prison every day when I was in school. As much as I loved people, I hated school because it was so restrictive, and I was always getting in trouble. It was almost like a fun-free zone, and I absolutely hated it with everything in me. You eat when you are told you can eat. You go to the restroom only when you have been permitted to go to the restroom. You enter and leave the doors of the school only when you have been accounted for and allowed to do so by the warden (and/or the principal). You speak when you are granted permission to speak, as so when asking questions. You shall not interrupt or disrupt, or you will be punished and sent to the warden's office (the principal's office). Universities and the mainstream media will trick you into believing that you must go to school, spend $40,000 plus on a college degree, and eventually, if you are lucky, get a good job with a good pension, and MAYBE if you are lucky, pay off all of the debt. If not, well, that is your fault for never being educated on how to become financially literate. Schools only teach students (a.k.a prisoners) how to get a job. They never teach you how to keep a job, and most certainly, schools will never teach you how to invent a job. This is why America is a nation of consumers and not producers.

 School never teaches that you have to unlearn what you are taught in school in order to become wealthy or truly successful in life. If you are not having a blast in life while also accomplishing your goals, then there is no point in even being alive. Better to have a small hut as you chase the relentless pursuit of happiness than an empire of anguish, authoritarianism, and anarchy - all thanks to regret and never pursuing true happiness. You must have fun at what you pursue, or there is no point in doing it. There will come a day when you are in your last moments of life, and you will wonder, "Did I really give everything I had? Did I accomplish my goals? And did I have fun doing it? What have I built for my children? Have I lived a good life, and am I happy with the way I lived it? Am I ready to close my eyes and meet my creator, knowing that I left everything on Earth with no regrets?" I can definitively say that even if my death were tomorrow, which one day will inevitably occur, I have truly accomplished everything that I have set out to accomplish, and I have done it my way completely and absolutely. "I had a lot of fun in my life." Will you be able to say the same? This is so important.

Now - make no mistake, although the feeling of satisfaction, success, and winning IS the most important result we can achieve in life if you can find a way to have fun on your way to the winner's circle, then you have truly mastered any who call themselves "happy" but not having fun while doing it. It is called the pursuit of happiness for a reason. We are all chasing happiness, but few will realize that happiness is something we can only pursue and capture for only a short time before it leaves our grasp again and again. Happiness is like chasing butterflies or catching fish.

We catch and release it, then chase the same result for the feeling of gratification and satisfaction over and over again. Happiness is a state of emotion based on gratitude, and our perception of the world, forwarded by a fluctuation of positive or negative events that continuously occur throughout our lives. Because of this primal and an unchallenged fact of life, you may as well have fun living while you're winning in the meantime while simultaneously pursuing happiness - the most powerful and satisfying outcome to an intended goal or adventure. Like the butterfly or the fish, happiness is the same. We catch, then we release, and we continue to chase the same feeling of gratification and satisfaction until we catch it again. That brings us to why I loved playing video games, making deals, and working out, which helped to fuel this desire.

Playing video games taught me to relax and enjoy brief periods of mental stimulation while also developing stronger hand-eye coordination. Making deals taught me how to sell, which is a critical asset in life and one that cannot be overlooked if you ever want to be successful at anything, and especially wealthy at some point along the way. If you can't sell, then you can't succeed. But of course, above all else, I enjoyed having fun in school because, after all, what else are Middle School and High School really for? It is not for getting straight A's, following all the rules, kissing ass, never making mistakes, playing everything safe, and appeasing your teachers. School is for fun and learning the social cues needed to thrive in a civilized society. School is for learning the bare minimum in efforts to later get a job you probably won't enjoy and, hopefully, paying off your bills before you die working until 64 with nothing to show for it.

Choose to let loose and have fun while chasing and accomplishing your dreams - and remember - be careful who you surround yourself with along the way. It only takes one wrong friend and one wrong move to ruin the course of your entire life. Remember this, especially if you ever plan to become a police officer.

Although I was indeed friends with everyone, known for being a prominent athlete and fairly popular, there were many times that I made my mom scared to death. There were many instances where I was suspended, given detention, and outside of school, nearly dying because of the stupid choices I had made with my friends. This is why I felt so inclined to write this chapter in this book. Surrounding yourself with friends who are constantly getting into drugs, drinking, getting in trouble with the law, and spending all their leisure time going to concerts and blowing their money, will result in you eventually following in the same footsteps. You must be so careful about who you choose to share your time with. Be so careful about who you allow to influence your decisions and better judgment. Be wise and discerning of your friends and environment because if you are not, and if you are not careful, you can easily find yourself losing out on your dream of becoming a police officer.

Some of the kids I graduated with in my police academy were always very careless about their decisions. I remember they would constantly go out to bars, drink, and post inappropriate videos on social media while completely incriminating themselves and leaving themselves vulnerable to exploitation. I, of course, would begin to do the same as I began to become like the people I hung out with.

I discerned that even when I was surrounded by cops, many of the cops I was surrounded by were also not the greatest people to surround yourself with. Many were stupid, careless, foolish, and downright oblivious to their own actions, truly believing they were invincible. I have known cops who later became fired cops because they chose to drink and drive after a night with their high school friends (many of whom were drug addicts or criminals themselves). It isn't my intention to bash Law Enforcement, but rather to warn future officers about the very real nature of any profession in general. Not every police officer is a Saint, and not every police officer is the Devil. It is a reality you will see in any career. Whether that career is Law Enforcement, politics, blue-collar work, laboratory focus, or entertainment… you name the industry… each one brings good and bad influences. Be careful about who you decide to surround yourself with and, most importantly, who you intend to be. How will you be remembered by those you associate yourself with? Will you be a leader or a follower?

My friends in school always consisted of a very broad circle of cliques. Being an All-State baseball player, football player, and powerlifter, I was always fairly popular. My primary clique was usually with the jocks but also with what people would describe as the "nerds." I enjoyed surrounding myself with the smartest people because I knew they could teach me things I didn't know, and they were generally the most loyal friends. I enjoyed learning from those who knew more than me. In my eyes, this was a blessing, and it was free. Many of the jocks were members of other social cliques as well, and vice versa to other cliques in school and in college. Some were country boys and rednecks (for the most part), some were members of the nerd clique, some were part of the preppy goody-two-shoes class, the goths, the introverts, and even the teacher's pets. In general, the school was basically a division of two classes of people - the Socs and the Greasers - I preferred to be right in between and friends with all.

In conclusion, you must be wary and cautious of who you choose to allow into your circle. Be careful who you trust, and be careful not to allow friendships to cloud independence and better judgment. Do not let peer pressure override your logic and reasoning, as this is the Achilles heel to any and all who seek to not only become police officers but also be successful in general. Be the leader of the pack.

Choose to be the one in the social group who is subtle, humble, charismatic, funny, loving, attractive, sociable, outgoing, quiet, constantly observing, and listening. Be strong in the convictions of your decision-making patterns, and be a master of your environment. If you can learn this important skill for success and power, then you will find yourself holding the responsibility of great success and power. Choose your friends ever so carefully, and be selfish in your journey to success. Friends will come, stay, and go. Be wise enough to let them. Lastly, be smart enough to be the influence rather than being the one who is influenced. If you ever seek to become a police officer, you must be ready to answer for who you have once associated yourself with. This knowledge is critical for all aspects of success, not just in Law Enforcement, but in any profession or trade.

Chapter 5: Relationships - Be Careful Who You Date

This is one of the most important chapters in this book. In being a police officer or anything in life, you have to choose the right mate, and you have to be carefully selective about it. You have to be selfish and put yourself first. Dating, and especially marrying the wrong woman, can ruin your life faster than you can blink. It takes one wrong decision and lack of judgment for you to destroy the path of your future. You have to be careful. If you're a female reading this book, the same goes for you. You have to choose the right man, the right mate, and here is why.

The reason this is so important is because whoever you end up with will share the outcome of your future with you. If you marry a woman who doesn't align with your long-term goals, or if you marry a woman who shares different political views, this can destroy any relationship and, of course, a marriage too. If you marry a woman who doesn't want kids and you do, that is a relationship built for imminent disaster and failure. If you marry a woman who goes to the club when you prefer to stay at home, that is a relationship built for failure. If you marry a woman who is clingy and dependent on your attention all the time, when you are laid back and independent, this is a relationship that is built for failure. If you marry a woman who enjoys spending every penny and never saving or investing her money while you value saving and investing your money, this is a relationship doomed for failure and entropy.

I myself have dated enough women in my lifetime to know better. I have dated some of the most beautiful women I ever knew personally. I learned how to talk to girls and pursue them aggressively without fear from my father. In fact, this is one of the few lessons I did learn from my father, aside from playing pool and being respectful to everyone I encountered. I have learned from my own mistakes, lack of judgment, and gaps of wisdom.

I broke the heart of the first love I ever had back in High School. She was the most beautiful girl in our school and one of the smartest. She was about my height, had brown hair, was Italian, and was an exceptional dancer. Today, she is a Forensic Pathologist and still just as beautiful. I cheated on this girl when I was 16. Here I had waited forever to date her, since third grade, and I messed it all up. She was the love of my life throughout half my time in school up until my Freshman year when she was finally allowed to date. When she was, I screwed up, broke her heart, and ruined a good thing - a pure thing, and worst of all. I broke her heart twice.

Fast forward one year later, and I began dating a blonde girl who had moved from a nearby town, and of course, I broke her heart too, just so I could eventually find myself dating that same girl I had always chased since third grade. After the first breakup, we began talking again while we were both in relationships. But this was just talking. Eventually, I ended up breaking it off with the blonde girl from the nearby town and reignited the fling with the first-ever "love of my life." Like the first time, I blew it and lost her a second time. That was the last time she ever trusted me, and we never dated again after this, no matter how hard I continued to try to get her back. Even up to college, I continued to pursue her until I finally realized it was never going to happen. I had blown it too many times. This is the price of falling victim to the chase and devaluing a woman by cheating. You deserve to get burned just like you burned her. I accepted my karma when years later, I received the other side of the bill.

After years of continuously pursuing my first love and trying to make up for the many foolish mistakes I made, I had given up on the chase for her forgiveness and trust. I never expected her to forgive me anyways. After all, I had developed a reputation for being a player and an untrustworthy guy to date, so why would she trust me? She had no reason to, and I accepted that fully.

Months later, I was dating a cheerleader from a town about 20 minutes from my hometown. This girl lived in Richmond who was a rival of our football team for years. I went to a playoff game with a football buddy of mine, and this girl asked me for my phone number. The next thing I knew, we were dating for about six months, and I eventually broke her heart too. I felt horrible, but I figured if it wasn't going to work out, I might as well let her know right away. This was a lesson learned that you should never lead a girl on, as it can truly hurt them. She hated me for a long time, but I like to think that maybe she has forgiven me. I haven't heard from her in many years now, but I know she is well. She was always beautiful, charismatic, and full of life. I wish her the very best.

More or so, I just wanted to hold onto that amazing feeling of being with the girl I fell in love with in third grade, so I dated as many girls as I could and tried to make the relationships work. I went on the dates, bought them flowers, and did everything I could to properly put in all the effort required to make the relationships work. When I finally moved on, I ended up dating another girl in my school who I had actually learned some very important lessons from.

My next real girlfriend after dating other girls in my school for a brief time, on and off, I began dating a star softball player in my graduating class, with whom I had always been great friends for years. We were both looking to play sports in college, so we just clicked and ended up together. We were friends from the beginning. She was a curly-haired redhead and fairly popular since her move to my hometown, with a tenacious and attractive sense of humor. We were both competitive, good-looking, had a lot of similar interests, but also completely different personality types and had conflicting long-term goals. This became a major issue in our relationship when we found ourselves at different schools in different states.

Interestingly enough, she was best friends with the same blonde girl that had moved to our school from the nearby town. I know what you're thinking… "This guy is a real piece of shit," but truth be told, I am trying to be honest about my past so you can learn from my mistakes and never make the same ones in your own life. That same blonde girl from the nearby town is doing very well for herself and very successful. It is important to note that the women I talk about in this chapter are not discussed as a point of insult or conjecture but as learning points and lessons for you, the reader. This chapter is about picking your relationships wisely, not leading girls on, not cheating, and being present in every relationship while also putting yourself and your goals first.

The curly-haired redhead had moved from the same nearby town as the blonde. They were best friends at the time. The redhead and I had been friends since she had moved to our school, but later, we found ourselves dating after realizing how alike we actually were, despite our many differences. We dated for about a year before eventually breaking it all off after an ugly last few months.

After graduation, we both had scholarships to play sports in college. She had a full ride at a community college in Ohio when I had signed to play football and baseball at Olivet College, a small, low-population, NCAA division 3 college in the heart of Michigan, just 35 minutes Southwest of Lansing. The relationship was up and down for that year together until we were apart and tried to make the long-distance thing work. As you could guess, it didn't work out at all.

We argued a lot but also had a blast with each other. Mostly though, it was arguing and constantly being at war with each other. This was primarily because we did not trust each other whatsoever - and trust is everything. We were always both suspicious and untrustworthy towards each other since we were both known to be devilish in our relationship pasts. We both knew this. She was very much a hypercompetitive, free-spirited, extroverted, and party girl, while I was a hypercompetitive, boring, introverted, and self-sufficient student-athlete who hated going to parties. It was safe to say that we were both the jealous types in those years, and it showed.

We were both a power couple while also a disaster couple at the same time. We were fire and ice. Like Batman and the Joker, we were a similar proportion of chaos, adventure, strength, danger, unpredictable nature, intention, vision, and excitement. Ultimately, we ended the relationship after enough Facetimes went South, and enough phone calls ended with an abrupt hangup. The arguing had become so bad that it was foolish to keep the roller coaster going any longer. There came a day when we just suddenly stopped texting, calling, or even looking at each other's social media pages any longer. Hurting each other and being in fear of the unknown became irrelevant and a waste of time for both of us. We both eventually knew that it was toxic and never going to work. Today, we are both friends and have made our peace with one another. She is also doing very well in her life today.

 Fast forward another year, and I recovered after another relationship had ended. Of course, I got myself into another relationship. I mean, what could one expect? I was in college, playing two sports, and surrounded by beautiful women everywhere. Not to mention, I was miserable and bored out of my mind going to many of the classes I went to, quite honestly, learning mostly useless information. Being able to flirt was the one incentive to actually go to class, tolerate the radical leftist jargon spewed by the professors and students, and still dress like you gave a damn, besides doing your best to stay eligible for sports and not flunk out of course. Girls were all you had as a male on a radically leftist, brainwashed college campus.

 The next girl I dated was the worst of all the girls I dated. Truth be told, it was downright just a mistake. She was extremely needy, clingy, obsessive, bipolar, rude, and…. Well… kinda crazy, to be frank. She was beautiful, of course, but crazy. She had brown hair, brown eyes, and a nice figure. Her mom was one of the bookstore cashiers on our campus. We had kicked it off well until she began spamming my phone and depending on me to constantly be her shoulder to cry on. Don't get me wrong. I have never had a problem being that guy for any girl I dated. That is what a man should do, but she was completely reliant on me for every facet of happiness and contentment in her life. That is beyond normal. She was not independent, and she did not have that spark of a strong, independent, and motivated woman that most of my exes shared. Needless to say, I learned that although, as a man, you should be glad to be a woman's rock and shoulder to cry on, you should also strive to be with someone who can take care of themselves without you in their life.

Choosing an emotionally and mentally strong woman means that she will be emotionally and mentally strong throughout any problem that occurs in life - whether those problems be minor arguments, the egregious process of pregnancy, the death of a family member, financial struggles, employment challenges, parenting complications, health discrepancies, or goal-oriented issues. Being able to endure these problems with your spouse is the characteristic of a strong partner, regardless of whether it is a man or woman. In a relationship, you are a team. Your mate should be strong and willing to take on any battle with you, by your side, or without you. That is a compatible mate and one worth keeping.

My next girlfriend was a gorgeous blonde-haired gal that moved from West Florida to Michigan. I remember her looking exactly like Carry Underwood. She was stunningly attractive. She was a bartender at Applebees at this time, and she was four years older than me. She was 23 years old when I was only 20 and still just a Sophomore in college and playing football and baseball. I met her at Planet Fitness in Battle Creek, Michigan. She was a self-sufficient, pot-smoking, beer-drinking, working girl. Normal, cool, and we got along really well. However, she was very skittish and did not trust anyone that well. This never bothered me, considering I was the same way. It was a healthy relationship that lasted about three months. It was fun because I remember this same girl buying me a beer because I was too young to buy it for myself at the time. She even bought me a few beers when we went out on our first date, and for some reason, I never got carded. Yes, I get it; as a cop, how dare I do something so reckless and dumb - but as I explained in the previous chapter, you have to live life and gain experiences, so you have stories when you're old.

Unexpectedly, at around the three-month mark, this same girl broke up with me because she believed that I had been talking to other girls when that was not the case. I had grown out of the cheating stages after learning my lesson from my first love. Again, another case of trust becoming a major factor in a relationship. I didn't think much of this, as I knew she had a troubling past to begin with and issues relating to her family. I respected her decision and moved on. At this point in my life, I knew it was time to just stay single for a while and stay focused.

For the next few years, up until I finally made it to the police academy, I was single and remained focused on my own success. I went to class and got good grades for the Criminal Justice portion of my college major, and in the meantime, I became a Freelance writer for a local newspaper, a weight room supervisor, and an author, and began educating myself on the confounds of starting businesses. I remember the movie "The Social Network", starring Jesse Eisenberg, being my motivation to start my own business. So, for years, I made money from starting what one could call "small businesses" or side hustles. I was making money driving drunk college kids back home from Frat parties and sororities. I was making money from selling t-shirts on Etsy that I designed. I did anything I could to find creative ways to make money, and somehow, I found myself making a killing.

Years later, when I found myself in the police academy, I dated a blonde girl from that academy for a short time. This was the second academy that I attended. We hit it off for a while. We were practically partners throughout the entire academy and sat by each other anyways, so, at some point, I made the first move and officially made her my girlfriend after we both graduated and passed the state exam. We also both had similar interests. Deep down, a large part of me knew it was never going to last, but I wanted to see if it could, considering we were both going to be cops. I figured, why not? We got along great and had a lot of fun dates. We would go to the academy, suffer together, and then, at the end of the day, get a drink at a bar just outside of our academy campus. It was fun while it lasted, but it wasn't true love.

Unfortunately, we were both different in too many ways and had different long-term goals. Not to mention, she did not want kids, and I did. That, for me, was the biggest deal breaker. She was also very flirtatious towards other men, controlling, argumentative, and combative. She was a girl that I knew I would never be able to trust indefinitely, and she had felt the same about me at a certain point. Trust, again, became the dealbreaker in this relationship. Not to mention, she was immature after this breakup. She slandered me in our academy group chat and constantly insulted anything I said in the chat. It wasn't long before I was suddenly ignored in the chat all of a sudden by the very peers I had helped to reach success in the academy, teaching them the ropes of what I had learned from the previous academy. I felt very betrayed and couldn't believe it.

It later became obvious that the relationship was going to be a repeat of the relationships I had mentioned before. So because of this, I ended the relationship and refused to lead her on. I did my best to remain civil, but eventually, I found myself blocking her, as again, I could not trust her - especially since she was another police officer and could ruin my career and my life with one lie if she wanted to. I did the smartest thing; I blocked her from all avenues and severed all ties with an ex for the very first time in my life.

This brings me to the woman I am still with today and the love of my life. The most beautiful, patient, understanding, independent, self-sufficient, strong, confident, trustworthy, and loyal woman I had ever come to meet. She is the one that was brave enough to choose me, and I am most proud to have chosen her. She is the strongest woman I have ever come to know and the most brilliant.

Believe it or not, I met her in March of 2022. She was sweet, kind, good-looking, cool, beautiful as could be, and motivated. I was immediately attracted to her. She was perfect. We had the same long-term goals. She had a healthy mindset and was actually three years younger than me. She was still in college when I had finally graduated from the police academy, gotten hired as a sheriff's deputy, and later hired as a small-town police officer. The moment I knew she was the one, however, was when she stayed with me throughout my time in the second police academy. At the end of my relationship with the girl from my academy, I began talking to her. She was everything the girl from the academy wasn't.

She was supportive, trusting of me, and I trusted her the same. She also respected me, respected my dreams, and never gave up on me when I was a struggling rookie cop, having to resign from my first department. She never left. Even when I had explained to her that she was free to leave if it was all too much for her to handle, she never left. This brings me to the most important lesson in this chapter - stay with those who believe in you. Never leave those who are truly loyal to you and who respect you as a human being and partner.

Out of the women I have dated, which is many, I had never met one like her. It was like she was an angel sent by God just for me, as Robin Williams stated in Good Will Hunting. I was perplexed by her loyalty and commitment to me, despite my ups and downs as a rookie cop and also a risk-taking entrepreneur and author. She was always supportive. She was the perfect mate and a woman I could not wait to call the mother of my kids.

In summary, there are many lessons in this chapter. If you are investing time into a relationship, be careful who you date. The wrong relationship can ruin your life if you are not careful. You will save years of your life and a lot of money on a potential divorce if you simply look for the following qualities in a spouse:

- Loyalty
- Trust
- Respect
- Overall Compatibility
- Common Interests & World Views
- Common Long-Term Goals
- Physical Attributes
- Mental/Emotional Attributes
- Spiritual or Religious Similarity
- Healthy Genes

These are the top 10 most important elements required if you are seeking to invest time into a relationship. Don't make the same mistakes I did. Don't break a woman's heart if you know you can live without them. Don't allow them to break yours, either. Be man enough, or woman enough, to value your future and be selfish for seeking the best partner and spouse that you deserve. The rest of your life depends on the partner you choose. Your mate is arguably one of the most important things in your life. You should elevate your spouse, and they should elevate you. You both should always be elevating each other and making each other better, never worse.

Who you choose to repopulate with, and spend the rest of your dying years with, is critical to accomplishing the combination of health, wealth, love, and happiness. If you choose the wrong partner, you could see your health, wealth, love, and happiness run away without you faster than you could imagine. I have seen it with friends, coworkers, and family members more times than I can remember. You must be so careful and diligent about the romantic relationships you choose to have. A marriage, especially, is a legally binding contract. It is a business partnership. You must think about this before you ever choose to settle down with someone who could potentially be the wrong person and the worst person for you. Be wise in your selection, and do not be afraid to be selfish in your search. It only takes one bad decision and one poor judgment of character to trap yourself into a life of bitterness, discontent, pain, trouble, problems, and regret.

Chapter 6: Becoming Financially Literate

It's important to note that I am not a financial advisor, nor have I earned any formal degree focused on financial advice. I'm not a C.P.A., and I am not an economist or financial expert. I am a business owner, investor, author, and police officer with life experience. In other words, I am an entrepreneur. I have read hundreds of books on the subjects of not only Criminal Justice but also finance, business, geopolitics, history, science, and life success.

I have learned how to master the concepts of not just saving money but also investing and making money work for me. I have failed my way to success through trial and error in many different business ventures. In my failures, I have learned that I was always rewarded when I found a way to turn my setbacks into successes.

Therefore, I added this chapter to give my own unique perspective on money management and how best to create a financial cushion as a police officer. These are just some of the suggestions and strategies that have worked for me in building my businesses and becoming financially free. I believe if you follow my blueprint, you will easily become wiser about how to manage your money in the long term. You need five basic ingredients in order to succeed in anything, and those are (1) Taking Action, (2) Persistence, (3) Consistency, (4) Speed, and (5) Information.

I felt it was an important chapter to add to this book because police officers, unfortunately, are some of the most financially illiterate players in the workforce. Some of us are very astute when it comes to financial literacy, but most are not. Truthfully, at the end of the day, Police Officers, quite honestly, get screwed financially. Same with military veterans in many cases. They risk their lives for extremely low pay. They sacrifice their time for the reward of saving others, but also, the risk of dying, and, you guessed it - extremely low pay. Although many police departments are beginning to pay police officers more deserved salaries, risking your life, in my opinion, is worthy of a minimal 6 figure salary at the least. There are many departments that pay less than $50k per year. I ask, why? Perhaps the consideration of supply and demand of police officers does come into play, but still - does it make sense? In this chapter, we explore the subject in its entirety.

I remember being on patrol one shift and listening to Robert Kiyosaki's "Rich Dad Poor Dad" audiobook on Spotify. I was working at my second police department at this time. Much of his lessons in that book have been recycled and relayed to you in this book. This is because Robert's book changed my life, and many of the lessons I learned from his book can easily change yours too.

I remember it was September of 2022. I had just turned 24. I had only been a police officer for about six months at this point, and honestly, I was starting to realize just how badly police officers got paid. I remember sitting in my patrol vehicle and running stationary radar when I listened to the part in "Rich Dad Poor Dad", where Robert Kiyosaki mentioned his Poor Dad working hard at his job as an educated teacher but always being disappointed when he would look at his paycheck the following week. It would never quite be enough to make ends meet, and it was always less than he would expect. Then, because he knew he was making such little money, he would cling to that money and store it away until he was dead and could no longer use it. Poor Dad's philosophy for money was, "Work hard, get a PhD., get a good job with a good pension, and save your money. One day, if you play life safe, you'll have a decent retirement".

The story of Robert's Poor Dad was very relatable for me, as I had been starting to feel the same way as Robert's Poor Dad. I was working five days a week, taking overtime whenever I could, slaving, and doing my best as a young cop - and still, I was unsatisfied and unable to enjoy my life. It always seemed like it was never good enough. When I was a cop, I felt like I was walking on eggshells, and felt like I could lose my job for anything because, as a police officer, you really can easily lose your job for anything, even if was something as small as a joke you accidentally let slip over your body cam for the prosecutors to hear. You are always one step away from poverty as a full-time cop with only one stream of income. Although I loved being a police officer, once I had done it for that brief six months, I suddenly wanted more in life. So I began chasing.

I had this recurring vision. I wanted the freedom to wake up at 10 a.m. every day of the week in a nice house that I owned. My personal debts would be paid off. I would make a cup of coffee, listen to the Morgan Stanley Market Update, run my businesses, order stuff I liked on Amazon because I could, get a workout in maybe, play nine holes of golf, go to the batting cages, join a Jiu Jitsu dojo, and spend the rest of my day doing whatever I wanted - how I wanted. To me, that was the idea of a comfortable and pleasant life.

I wanted the freedom to spontaneously pack up the car and go to a random place on the globe for a random vacation. I wanted the time to be able to write and pitch my screenplays. I wanted time to learn how to play piano, guitar, and saxophone again (yes, before joining football, I was first chair Saxophone and pretty good on the strings). What I'm saying is I wanted time to spend with my friends, time to spend with my family and my mom, and time to spend with my girlfriend. Perhaps more than anything else, I wanted time to look for real estate deals and build my businesses. I wanted to grow an empire and expand my name and wealth. It was personal for me. I hated feeling shackled because I was making little money and working all the time rather than building my empire and becoming financially free. I knew it was time to change.

Law Enforcement was rewarding, but for me, I quickly got burnt out from the job. I always thought to myself, "Is this really the best I can do?" I had seen my fix of action, blood, gore, death, and close calls. I wanted Freedom, comfort, options, and of course, to be rich - much like Robert Kiyosaki mentioned in "Rich Dad Poor Dad." I wanted an everyday routine that was convenient, pleasant, fun, and challenging yet simple, systematic, and within my own control. I wanted this in all areas of life. Health, Wealth, Shelter, Food/Water, Family, Love, and Happiness. Balance in life brings beauty and harmony. Imbalance brings chaos, disorder, discontent, poor health, and poverty.

Why did I become an entrepreneur when I already became everything I wanted to be since I was a kid? Why sacrifice a steady, solid, and beloved career for a dream just to make more money? Well, it's simple. I wanted more out of life, and I wanted to help the world in a more indirect but highly effective way - which was real estate investing and becoming an entrepreneur. I have been an entrepreneur since I can remember. It's always been in my blood. In being an entrepreneur, you can change the entire world, and the limitations to your success and wealth are uncapped. You can go as high as you want and as big as you want. The cards are in your favor in a world where few hold the powerful status of wealth and control over their own destiny. The cards are in your favor when the world is too afraid to even act and too afraid to even work with the hand life gave them.

In being an entrepreneur, I could help the world in much bigger ways. I could provide shelter by working as a landlord in the hospitality (real estate) business. I could provide real-life value and priceless information to millions of people by publishing books such as the one you are reading now. I could donate to charities and raise money for real, long-term, powerful causes and ideas that make people's lives better. I could create a chain of businesses that provide timeless, valuable, in-demand, and universally desired services, much like Amazon has done. I could have podcasts, websites, stores, automation chains, and sales funnels so I could become my own bank. Of course, this is because anything that is timeless - is priceless. Time is our greatest asset. Time is the only asset that has no limit to its price.

The truth of it is I was sick of exchanging my time and security for money as a cop and getting little in return for it all around. Investing, and the idea of making money while I slept, seemed much more intelligent, reasonable, and logical. The way I saw it, as a cop, we were good at wearing many hats, to begin with. Why not take advantage of such a skill and use it to build a better, more prosperous life for myself and others? How could I find a way to be of service to people while doing so proactively? I knew at that point I wanted more in life financially. I was going to become an investor rather than a common cash saver and 401k/pension pusher. I was going to learn how to make money work for me, so I would no longer have to work for money. Simply put - I want to have the CHOICE to work. I don't want to HAVE to work. This is the mindset that every entrepreneur has, and it only makes logical sense to think in such a manner.

I respect my time far too much to sell all of my time to work until I die. Although I am proud to serve my country and to make a difference in today's unpredictable world, I am also a strong believer that you must create a future of financial freedom for your own family so they can live a good life. Some carry the philosophy of working to live, while some believe in living to work. In the meanwhile, the wealthy are sitting outside of the chessboard, being held up by the working class, who do all of the heavy lifting for the royalty of today's age - the business owners and investors. In the end, in today's day and age, the wealthy are the business owners and investors. The entrepreneurs. They are like royalty. Real estate literally means "Royalty." Those are the wealthy business owners and investors today. They control the game, and they control the fate of humanity while building their empires - using the working class and consumer market to do all of it. This has always been the way the world operates.

The wealthy and financially free can very much control the course of information and even mankind's ultimate evolution. Like it or not, history has proven that having wealth, influence, and control over the masses are the fundamental building blocks to holding TRUE power. As a police officer, do you want to have power over the enforcement of the Law or power over all aspects of life? Power over your own life, financially, is very important. Securing this in their own lives is a goal every officer, or any person in general should seek to obtain.

So why am I droning on about all of this? While finding and keeping a job is prioritized by the 99%, creating jobs is prioritized by the imaginative and the rule breakers - the wealthy who enjoy the 1%. The C students are classified as "average" in school, but they are far from average. The C students understand that school is unnecessary and temporary. They understand that school is important, but they won't let school control them. They do what they must to get through the schooling system so they can focus their time on building and creating the future. The C students build businesses and own the world. The B students work for the C students and hold some controlling interest, but not all of the control, of course. The B students are on the right track. They are similar but focus too much time and energy on getting good grades rather than focusing primarily on their own goals in life. The A students work for the B students and are the common workers and/or employees/professionals who are employed by the B and C students.

The witty, awkward, quirky, quiet kid in school who sits in the back of the classroom and says few words are usually the same ones who later hold the keys to power and wealth in life. They are the ones who are plotting world domination. They are looking for a way out of the rat race. That same awkward, quiet kid in the back of the classroom is plotting his success, imagining ways to sit atop the world and make it his throne.

Later, that same kid is the student who was greatly underestimated, commonly laughed at, and viewed as the crazy, whacky, often eccentric troublemaker. That kid later drops out of school, becomes invisible to those around him for the next ten years as he builds the foundation of his empire, and reappears God-like. That underestimated, imaginative, Sigma wolf eventually becomes the genius behind just one successful business, investment, or idea. Now, they are holding the world in the palm of their hand, pulling the strings on every action and inaction and every decision made - all because they found a way to become wealthy and buy their way to control, influence, and power.

At the first police department I worked as a rookie cop, which was a Sheriff's Department. I was making even less than I was making at my second department - just a small city police department working with a population of 3,000 people. I would get maybe 2 or 3 calls for service per shift, make around 3-4 traffic stops, and maybe write one citation. Every once in a while, I would arrest a drunk driver, chase a fleeing felon, or have to get physical with someone, but usually, it was a quiet night. It was an 8-hour shift and paid me $23 per hour. In my first department, I worked 12-hour shifts, and the starting pay was only $21 per hour. It wasn't until I left that department that they implemented a pay increase.

Is it really smart to be a police officer or soldier any longer than your community or country asks you to? When is enough service enough? Isn't it possibly more reasonable and logical to serve a necessary and rewarding amount of time as a police officer or soldier but to primarily focus on security, comfort, and financial independence? Is it really worth it to be micromanaged by your Sergeants and Lieutenants every single shift you work or tour that you serve? Just so that you can make peanuts compared to those who simply chose to become their own boss and become financially literate? Are your Sergeants and Lieutenants as happy as they appear with their own lives? Take a closer look at what you see. Are they truly happy and content with how much money they make and how much money they will have when they retire? This goes for any job where another human being has control over your life. Why should they get to dictate your future when you choose to vacation, make more money, take days off, or do your job in a way that you believe to be more effective?

I have found that in this profession of Law Enforcement, many cops think they are financially secure, but they are far from it. They are missing the key information and skills required in order to succeed in business and in other aspects of life. Many believe they are invincible and have it all figured out. Arrogance is common with us cops, as we believe we hold all of the answers and essential wisdom to success. Meanwhile, they are usually living in a house priced at around $200,000, with an average of 2-4 children running around, a spouse who makes around $60,000 per year, 2-3 vehicles they can't afford, and credit card debt up to their ears. They often do not have multiple streams of income. This is not every officer, but it is common, and I have seen it far too much. It isn't a bad life, but it isn't the best life either. It can be so much better.

Granted, this is obviously not always the case, and perhaps some police officers or veterans reading this book are already financially free. If so, then that is great, and I'm glad to hear that - but you should still take the time to hear another perspective on becoming financially free to enhance your own knowledge and skill base. I have started and run many successful businesses before ever entering the career of Law Enforcement. I know what it takes to be wealthy and to secure multiple streams of income.

I have always believed that it is a society's duty to take care of the elderly, their families, and the brave few who defend our Freedom. This is why I added this chapter. I want my fellow police officers and our brave military Veterans to be able to live life financially free. I want single moms in the world who struggled like my mom growing up to secure financial freedom. I want the elderly to enjoy their final days living the way they want to live and deserve to live.

Making money work for me is what allowed me the opportunity to write this book and become free in all areas of life, such as wealth, shelter, food/water, love, and health. I am not a financial guru or a billionaire (yet), but I do live a very satisfying life today, and I managed to find a way to become wealthy without having to work that hard for it. I learned how to be rich by simply turning hobbies into assets. This way of thinking, and the respect for entrepreneurship and the American Dream, will inevitably change your mindset and allow you to become truly financially literate. This means no more 401ks, Roth IRAs, or saving habits you might have learned from Dave Ramsey. Like Wikipedia, Dave Ramsey is a good starting point for obtaining a financially free lifestyle. Financial Freedom means saving up only until you can invest and make money work for you. You have to learn how to deploy assets like bullets in a machine gun. This means unlearning what Dave Ramsey has taught you and transitioning to the language and knowledge taught by the 1%.

When you have saved enough money, you have to elevate your knowledge from the Dave Ramsey mindset to the Robert Kiyosaki mindset. You have to know what you are getting into, and you have to be willing to do one of two options:

Option 1) Sacrifice all of your other childhood dreams if you want to be a police officer for a 10-20 year career or longer. Dedicate your life fully to Law Enforcement and commit everything to it (If Law Enforcement wasn't your dream, to begin with.)

Option 2) Create a financial plan to obtain security, comfort, and wealth so you can accomplish those dreams and goals within the next decade and, if desired, still be a police officer part-time. Best of both worlds.

Both options provide a choice. One option provides the choice of being an employee and a lifetime police officer, and one option provides the choice of being a police officer and accomplishing those other big dreams you always imagined possible as a kid. But truly, you have to decide which path is your path.

Having a professional career requires one to be just that - a consummate professional and to carry themselves appropriately, accordingly, and in diamond-clear fashion 24/7, 365 days a year. As a police officer, you have to live your life like a camera is always on you - because in this profession, there is literally always a body camera on you. You should live like a camera is always on you every single day, regardless of your chosen profession. Chances are, when you are least expecting it, your every move is being recorded and documented. You are always being watched - whether it be by your fellow man or God himself.

Know what you are getting into, and understand that if you seek to become wealthy, then becoming a police officer will make that goal much more challenging. If you truly want to become a police officer and a wealthy individual whose money works for them, then you will have to take the route that I took to become wealthy, using different assets to support my lower wages earned as a police officer. Having several different streams of income is critical to building a future of financial freedom. It is financially intelligent to have several different, often unique, streams of income.

The average millionaire has seven streams of income. The seven different streams of income are categorized as (1) Earned Income (any job requiring you to fill out a W2 form), (2) Interest Income, (3) Profit Income, (4) Dividend Income, (5) Capital Gains Income, (6) Royalty Income, and (7)

Rental Income. Millionaires invest in assets more than liabilities and impulse purchases. The fact is, cops just don't have seven streams of income on average, and from my experience, cops are pretty horrible with how they spend/save their money. Here's why.

We cops are, overall, a clique of middle-class, blue-collar, usually ex-military, alpha personality types, and very, very, very, very cocky. However, police officers are very feeble-minded and blind in many ways too. Despite police officers being capable of investigating highly dangerous and traumatic situations and solving complex problems, police officers have this way about them... almost like nothing you tell them is something they don't already know better than everyone. Police officers gossip like a high school cheerleading team. I would argue that less than 5% of them are living in the upper class.

A police officer is a great thing to be. However, police officers remain poor because they are indoctrinated into believing that a 401k, pension, and Roth IRA are the greatest means of becoming wealthy, and having a stable retirement, when in reality, 401ks, pensions, and IRAs are one of the greatest ways to stay poor until you're dead and left with nothing but a 0 balance - IF YOU'RE LUCKY.

I was investing my earned income into four separate assets when I first started out as a cop at 22 years old. I invested in everything I could. I hardly spent any money when I was a police officer unless it was used to build my businesses or pay for basic weekly necessities like gas and food. Mainly, this is because I didn't make enough anyways, but also because I wanted to eventually add real estate and my small business to my asset column.

It took a lot of saving up before I could finally add real estate to my asset column. Before I had ever gotten into real estate, I was more concerned with finding a way to consistently pay off a monthly mortgage for my first property. Since Law Enforcement was hardly doing this for me, I knew I had to find other ways to finance my goal of becoming a real estate investor as a side hustle.

When I saved up ten grand, I went all in on starting my own ATM business, as I knew that ATMs provided a greater potential ROI than real estate. Despite the reality of the U.S dollar dying and the banking system dying, I believe that ATMs will still be in use up until at least 2025. I knew that if I did things fast enough, then I could certainly generate a good means of passive income in order to pay for my main investment goal, which was real estate. I figured that if one ATM in a decent, high-traffic location could generate anywhere from $500-$1,200 per month ($6,000 to $14,000 per year), then 10 of those ATMs could create $5,000-$12,000 per month ($60,000 to $144,000 per year). That is real money, and that was a good enough reason for me to start that business. Unfortunately, however, this business hardly made any money, as it did appear to be another failed business after falling for the hard sell from Instagram gurus. But it was still great practice.

It took me less than $500 and 48 hours to form my LLC business entity and obtain a business bank account. The hardest part of starting my ATM business was finding site locations, as I had a cold called nearly 100 businesses before finally getting a "Yes" to the point of getting my first contract signed. My eventual goal was to get into the Bitcoin ATM game, as obviously, cryptocurrencies were clearly going to be the future. But this never happened. I quickly focused my ambitions on investing every cent I could get into real estate. The ATM business became a business I always kept around in case I ever did get lucky enough to land a site location.

Primarily, at 22-23 years old, I was invested in cryptocurrency for the most part, and my 401k was attached to my earned income (Law Enforcement). When I was 24 years old, I transformed my asset class into cash, crypto, gold, my podcast "The Brendan Ecker Influence," real estate, and the ATM business I never wanted to give up.

Truthfully, I never considered my 401k, or any kind of pension, an asset. Mainly, this is because a 401k or pension could've never possibly earned me the same R.O.I (Return on Investment) that owning a rental property or business could have within a 10-20 year time frame - and time is the greatest asset above all.

Not only that, but the government basically had full control over my money when I was contributing to a pension/401k plan. If I wanted to take the money out before I was 53 years old, I would be penalized (EVEN THOUGH IT'S MY MONEY, TO BEGIN WITH - that is called white-collar crime). That didn't sit well with me. I needed a better way to become wealthy fast and properly.

I remember all of the fellow cops I graduated with being so reliant on the promise of a lousy pension or 401k. They drooled and marveled over the recruiters when they would give their pitch for their department pensions or 401ks. I would simply laugh in my head. The kids I graduated with were just that - kids still - even the 45-year-olds. They had the financial literacy of 8th or 9th graders. They were like hamsters on a hamster wheel, chasing a hanging crumb on a string - so motivated to get that little crumb, all only to be dissatisfied and having wasted a lot of energy and time in the process.

I'll never forget how smart the kids in my police academies felt simply because they had managed to get hired at a department that had a "2.5 multiplier" for their "great pensions." I remember how attached they were to the idea of earning a "great pension." All they would have to do is a slave at the same police department they started working at for 20-30 years, and if they were patient enough and fortunate enough to live that long, AND if they had not chosen to move to another department in that same 20-30 years, then they would get to enjoy their pensions (which would likely be between $300,000 to $1,000,000 if they were lucky).

Despite this sad truth, many of the kids I graduated with were strong in their convictions like me and unwilling to change their perspectives, and that's okay. It never bothered me that my peers would often disagree with me on the subject of retirement and which way of getting there was best. They were just as young as me. But even I could discern that they were too young to be so boring in regard to their financial visions. None of them knew how to think big. None of them had dreams and goals that were larger than life. I remember just one cadet in my academy owning his own woodworking business and having a passive side hustle. That same cadet was a prior DOD employee before becoming a cop. He later moved to Florida with his family and is doing very well for himself today.

It was always the same kind of goals you would hear from cops. The common rookie police cadet was never interested in building businesses and creating an empire so they could help people in a more indirect, outward way, which I thought was irregular, for most kids were in their early 20s. I remember wondering if I was just immature, if I was more mature, or if I was just different in general. I never understood why there was this lack of vision and creativity in the job. For me, I needed this to keep a 9-5 exciting.

Everyone in my academy wanted to eventually become police officers at the federal level, or they wanted to be detectives or K9 handlers. It was always the same goal of making their way to the ranks of detective and Lieutenant at their respective departments. My goals were admittedly fairly similar but still larger than life, and I was an entrepreneur just as much as I was a police officer in my mind.

I wanted to save lives as a standard road patrol officer for about ten years and maybe, become a S.W.A.T. operator or a detective along the way. If I had accomplished those goals, I would be content. If I had not, I would still be content because my visions were always grander than simply being a police officer. I, of course, always wanted to be rich more than anything and to be able to provide generational wealth for myself and my family.

As my long-term goal, I wanted to build an empire. I wanted to be like Nathan Mayer Rothschild and John D. Rockefeller. I wanted to be like a bank for everyone. I wanted to build something life-changing and impactful. My 20-year goal was to eventually own a chain of subsidiary businesses that would help provide a financially independent life for my family and me and for the next five generations. I wanted to sell Hollywood screenplays, publish my books on the side, grow my real estate portfolio, and build/buy other attractive businesses that appealed to me through private equity channels. I wanted to not just build businesses but rather a powerful bloodline of successful and like-minded children. After all, what is the purpose of life if not to procreate and expand our genetics for the betterment of mankind's evolution? What is the purpose of life if not to explore, adventure, and discover new realms of dimensions, new capabilities of our species, and unlock secrets and portals to different worlds in this ever-expanding universe? In order to do this, we need strong generations of human beings who are taught to chase their dreams and accomplish what is believed to be impossible.

Eventually, I was able to do it all, and it was because I was financially literate by the time I graduated from college at just 21. It is so important to be financially literate if you want to be a police officer. You have to think bigger and not submit to the majority of those who cling to 401ks and pensions in Law Enforcement. Don't be a sucker for the government - especially when you are working as a member of the government. Throw yourself into the arena and compete to be Great. Gain the desire to swim with the sharks and run with the beasts. Escape from the Matrix or die by it.

Take risks and try new things outside of just being a police officer. Start a brand, write music, paint, sketch, or build something - but don't be afraid to fight against the current and take risks so that you can provide an extraordinary and prosperous life for your family.

As a police officer, use the tax laws to your advantage, do research on finance, and learn how to make passive income through real estate investing. If you fail to change the way you view money and how it works, you will continue to work for money until you die, and more likely than not, you will die, leaving your family in debt. There will come a day when you get sick or someone in your family gets sick. You should ask yourself, will you be able to pay for those medical bills, the house, and everything else they were helping you pay for? A 401k or pension will leave you penniless in the end, just as it does most Americans today. 401ks and pensions are outdated, and they only worked in the Industrial Era. Today, 401ks and pensions are useless liabilities for poor people who have no financial literacy. 401ks and pensions are worthless compared to assets like real estate, businesses, gold, silver, oil, cryptocurrency, and the most valuable asset - Time.

I remember always being frustrated because all of my peers from both police academies would laugh at me when I would tell them that pensions and 401ks were expendable, worthless, and no longer a trustworthy hedge for inflation and other retirement challenges. At this point, I was by no means wealthy or as financially literate as I am today, but I still knew that 401ks and pensions were not real ways to become wealthy or financially free. I always knew that real estate investing and building businesses were the easiest and fastest ways to build wealth and financial freedom. But obviously, at this time, I wanted to catch bad guys and save lives more than I did becoming a real estate investor. So I sucked it up. I would allow them to be wrong, and I would accept the fact that I could not break them out of their financially illogical and incorrect ways of thinking. Like most people, I learned that they would have to learn the hard way or on their own time.

They would call me a conspiracy theorist and laugh in my face when I would try to explain why 401ks and pensions were not good retirement resources anymore. They would call me crazy when I told them that I kept all my money in cash, real estate or R.E.I.T.S (Real Estate Investment Trusts), cryptocurrency, and gold. Today, I am the one who has gotten the last laugh. They are still slaving at their same police departments, chasing the lie of a "great pension" and "good 401k plan" while I am making money while I sleep.

The kids in my academies truly believed that a pension and 401k were the only ways to invest in your retirement. All because their parents had learned the same lessons from their own parents... thus, the cycle of poverty in America continues. They thought they were smart for investing in these ridiculous means of "retirement" and "passive income," when really, they get taxed the most for their 401ks and pensions, penalized the most for it, and given virtually zero tax deductions. But this did not matter to the kids in both of the consecutive police academies I graduated from. Every single one of them was so easily hypnotized and sold by the pitch of "getting paid to sit at home." I remember always thinking to myself, "Hmmm. Or I could just get paid to sit at home by owning rental properties. Why do I need a pension?" The moral of the story - 401ks and pensions are NOT the number one way to become wealthy, in my own personal opinion. Real estate, buying businesses, and investing in cryptocurrencies with utility are the answers.

Every fair-minded person should demand more and should seek a life of effortless financial comfort and independence, and that is why I felt this chapter was so important in your journey of becoming a police officer. You need to have something else to turn to after risking your life and earning a little under $70,000 a year (and F.Y.I... that salary depends on your department... it will usually take a few years to make anything above $60,000 per year). With a handful of rental properties, you could be doubling that salary and barely working at all.

A 401k or pension will never get someone to have financial freedom. If it does, I can guarantee it won't be before they are 40 years old in 90% of cases. The cold, sad, hard truth is that the only people who invest in 401ks and IRAs are the suckers and punching bags to the financially educated and intelligent. They are the little people and the ones who allow the rich to thrive. It is a cold, painful fact. They pay the most in taxes and earn the least on the charts (just like cops). They feel smart when they listen to Dave Ramsey when in reality, Dave Ramsey is a starting point for those who are trying to be financially educated. But even Dave Ramsey knows that his own advice is for those who want to live safely with money and for those who are trying to get out of debt. His information is based on those who are trying to learn about the basics, not about what Elon Musk, Bill Gates, Warren Buffet, or Jeff Bezos are doing. Those who are willing to take calculated, mature risks with their finances in order to compound their wealth in real ways are the same people who follow Robert Kiyosaki's Rich Dad, Poor Dad philosophy. I prefer to take necessary risks that catapult me to my intended destination in life, which is a place where I can afford to maintain my Wealth, Health, Love, Happiness, Time, and Freedom.

If you can learn and understand the language of the rich, then you'll suddenly be on your way to becoming not just a police officer but a wealthy police officer. I wanted to include this chapter to give you a new perspective on the future. I wanted to trigger you to think and consider where you believe your goals lie after hearing an alternative viewpoint from a guy who has been a police officer and experienced it.

If you choose to get into Law Enforcement, you will need to become financially educated so you can not just have a good retirement, but also provide for your family and live long enough to meet your grandchildren. As soon as you become a police officer and as soon as the hype of the job fades after about six months, things begin to feel very routine. I would get micromanaged by my Chief or Lieutenant for the same little things every week, and it began to become old and boring. I felt like a robot, and I felt like I was worthless. Even though I was helping people, I still felt like I wasn't helping enough people. I felt like there weren't enough people I was impacting. I wanted to accomplish so much more in life, even though I had already accomplished the grueling task of becoming a police officer. I remember constantly thinking to myself when I finally got hired and settled into the department I was meant to be in, "So… is this it? What happens now? I guess… make a traffic stop? Run some radar? Finish that Home Invasion report? Do a property check? I guess I just wait for something to happen like I did last time."

I had gotten burnt out, and I hadn't even been a police officer for one year. After handling enough domestics, shootings, robberies, and car accidents, the job got old fast for me. It lost the spark it had when I was in the academy, and I was just very intent on finding a way to quit my job and move on to things that truly interested me and made me passionate. I wanted to work for only a few years and spend the rest of my days doing what I wanted, when I wanted, how I wanted - simply because I had the money to afford it. That is what I was set on accomplishing from then on. This is why you must learn to be financially literate.

Chapter 7: Work Like a Cop, But Think Like a Business Owner

You've heard the term, "The borrower is a slave to the lender." Think about it for a minute. The borrower (the tenant) is a slave to the lender (the landlord). The landlord is a slave to the banks. Thus, this relationship is reliant upon one another. Under an LLC status, you now pay much less in taxes due to write-offs, deductions, and depreciation, and you have a growing relationship with the banks and mortgage companies. If you can find a way to use an LLC (preferably for real estate), then you can hedge against the chances of working a lifetime in Law Enforcement for a measly $5,000 per month when you do eventually retire at 45-60 years old. Or, even better, imagine having that $5,000 per month from your pension AND $10,000 per month coming in from your x20 single-family rental properties. The same benefits go along with owning a route of cash-flowing ATMs, which has a much higher ROI per month statistically, usually at around 30% over 15%.

As a landlord for a real estate business, you get a conventional loan from the banks on a 5-20% investment on the purchase price of a property (preferably something cheaper, and either a single or multi-family property) that you want to rent out to some willing tenants. The banks make their money back on the loan thanks to the rent paid off by the landlord. The landlord simultaneously makes a profit from the monthly rent paid by the tenants, and the tenants have a comfortable roof to lay their heads under when they fall asleep at night. Alas, you've provided a highly valuable service for moderate investment cost and minimal effort. Not only this, but you can now say that you are in both the crime-fighting business and the hospitality business.

Now, imagine that you own ten rental properties that generate a cash flow of $500 a month each. That's $5,000 a month when you add up all of those rents. In just one year, those ten rental properties that collect $500 every month will eventually generate an annual salary of $60,000. That's an upper middle class, a comfortable salary, all in exchange for very doable work and hours required. The same income will generally be found if you were to own ten cash flowing ATMs in high-traffic locations.

I chose to contribute 20% of my biweekly paycheck to the government's provided retirement plan, which was a 401a (basically a 401k) but realized immediately that I was getting suckered out of an extra $300 cash that I could be saving up to invest in real estate every month. So I went from contributing 20% of my biweekly paycheck into my 401k to contributing only 3.5% and collecting the extra $300 cash per paycheck - safe from the greedy hands of Uncle Sam and untaxed.

That cash that I would pump into my savings every paycheck was later used to start my ATM business and later buy my first rental property, which allowed me a life of financial freedom and the ability to retire early and live Free - which was not the same that I could say about most of the kids I went to High School, College, and the Police Academy with. Today, many of them are still working for money and working for someone else, risking their lives for little to no recognition or appreciation. I ask, why? If you're going to work, you should never work for money. You should be working for time and making your money work for you.

In the end, the way I see it... what's the point? After getting enough drunks off the street, arresting enough pedophiles, writing enough tickets, chasing enough felons, dodging enough bullets, being on shift during an officer-involved shooting, and dealing with the world's problems constantly - you learn that saving the world is never going to be a reality as a police officer. You could be a cop who has done the job for 30 years, and still, bad guys will always continue to fill the streets with or without you on duty. In fact, when I was working at my first department, the Sheriff's Deputy, who was one of my F.T.O's, made this point.

An F.T.O that I was with at the time, who was one of the more experienced deputies who had spent time with Flint P.D, S.W.A.T, and the Drug Task Force before his time as a sheriffs deputy at my department, is the same deputy who awakened me to the fact that it's impossible to save the world. This same deputy, who had glasses, a great sense of humor, but a gift for policing, was one of my more favored F.T.Os.

He was also the same deputy I did my first ride-along with years before I got hired at this department. He told me how he had been doing the job for 27 years. He told me how he had seen it all. He told me how he spent time on S.W.A.T, many years with the Drug Task Force, was a firearms instructor, an F.T.O, and a bodyguard for Brett Michaels (who this Deputy was obsessed with, might I add, although who could blame him)? I remember that same F.T.O. had said to me, "No matter how long you do this job, you're never gonna save the world. Trust me. I've been trying to find a way to save the world for the past 27 years. The bad guys will always be there to keep you busy. They always continue recycling back on the streets. When you find a way to save the world, let me know, kid."

To my amazement, I sat in the passenger seat that day as he was filling in for one of my other FTOs at the time, and I kept lingering on those words. It was a powerful statement to me, and it made me evaluate the career I had gotten myself into in many ways. It made me think about how I could actually save the world. Immediately, I thought to myself,

"Well, clearly, the best way to save the world isn't by being a cop." That was the moment I began wondering, "Hm. Maybe there's a better way to help people and make a greater impact. Maybe it's by doing something else." I began considering those influential human beings that I had always admired and learned from growing up, like Elon Musk, Warren Buffett, Jeff Bezos, Donald Trump, Robert Kiyosaki, and many others. I started wondering if it would be easier to save the world by making money and deploying it to push forward the human race.

The way I looked at it... money allowed me to fight crime and contribute so much more. I could use my wealth to lobby and donate to political organizations that cared about keeping the American Dream alive. I could use my wealth to amplify the belief and message of God and the Holy Spirit. I could use my wealth to promote the sanctity of marriage, love, compassion, personal growth, success, goal-oriented achievements, and the expansion of the human race as a whole.

In my mind, being a man of high net worth allowed me the opportunity to donate money to police departments, Criminal Justice training programs, police academies, colleges, veteran hospitals, homeless shelters, medical research organizations, the protection of the Amazon rainforest, humanity's exploration and colonization of Mars, the maintenance of today's far-leftist media networks, the development of charitable nonprofit organizations, the rebirth of quality, not quantity, Hollywood entertainment projects… you get the picture. Making money work for me, in my opinion, is a more powerful means of affecting change and influence rather than just making arrests, risking my life, and getting attacked by cowardly politicians for it.

Making money work for you, so you can use it to change the world for the better. It may not be sexy, but it's the sexier option of the two in terms of making a global impact. It is the more reasonable way to do so effectively, with strong, aggressive, game-changing investment. As a police officer, you have the power to make a local difference. As a wealthy, high-net-worth person, you have power. Having such power allows one to make a global difference and become a person of influence - the most significant and extravagant form of power known to the human race.

Becoming a person of both wealth and power, therefore allowing you to become a person of influence, is the most important form of power, especially - income. Influence is extremely critical to reaching limitless success in today's economy, which is an attention economy. You have to be influential in order to rise above the masses and stake your claim in the world. You have to be a person of influence if you want to network with other influential people. Influence is a characteristic of leadership. Influence allows a path to accomplish any and all goals that you wish to achieve because you gain access to other influential people and the hearts and minds of the masses. So before getting into Law Enforcement, ask yourself - "Do I want to be wealthy, or do I want to be a police officer? Do I want to make a difference locally, or do I want to make a difference globally? Do I want to be influential to a few, or do I want to be influential to the masses?"

In order to accomplish these tasks simultaneously, and before getting hired into a department, it will take either inheriting wealth and keeping it, continuing an ongoing successful business, or following this advice and using it at your own will so you can grow and learn from my successes and failures, as well as my training and experience in life, and in Law Enforcement. This is why, like all multimillionaires, you should have more than seven streams of income at one time.

At the time this book was written, I had four streams of income and was holding a total of 7 different assets in September of 2022. The seven total assets I was holding at this time were:

1. Cash
2. Cryptocurrency
3. Gold
4. Real Estate
5. Screenplays
6. Autobiographies
7. E-Commerce

When I was on patrol and sitting stationary radar with nothing to do, instead of listening to music on the radio, I was listening to The Wall Street Journal, Morgan Stanley Financial News, and the Goldman Sachs market updates. I would religiously learn from the Bigger Pockets Real Estate Investing Podcast, the Investors Podcast, Tax-Free Living, The Game, and Hustlers University. I was consuming content from investors and business minds such as Andrew Tate, Kris Krohn, Grant Cardone, Tai Lopez, Alex Hormozi, Gary Vaynerchuck, MrBeast, and so many other successful entrepreneurs.

I was consuming content from channels like the Billionaires Podcast and the Rich Dad Radio Show. I was continuously filling my brain with the language of money from Wall Street titans like Peter Schiff and Ray Dalio. I revered the financial minds of capitalists who changed the world, like Elon Musk, Jeff Bezos, Mark Zuckerberg, Bill Gates, Warren Buffett, George Soros, the Rockefellers, the

Rothschild Family, the Carnegies, J.P Morgan, Dr. Michael Burry, Mark Baum, and players like the Lehman Brothers. I learned from pretty much anyone who could teach me how to think and compete with the best entrepreneurs and investors on the planet. I would dive into the rabbit hole and find any information I could get on the top investors in New York City, Los Angeles, Dubai, Singapore, and Hong Kong.

I listened to nothing but business, finance, banking, real estate, geopolitics, history, and wealth-building audiobooks to build my knowledge base outside of my primary area of specialization, which was Law Enforcement. This is mainly because in the police academy, they had 40 different departments that would come into a recruit, and all they would talk about is the common middle-class jargon of pensions, 401ks, and retirement after twenty years of slaving at the same job. It was like becoming rich was never in the cards when the recruiters would speak to us. There was no good advice on how to start businesses, compound wealth, and become rich enough to retire after maybe 6-7 years of hard work in the job - which is what I was aiming for in Law Enforcement.

I was constantly learning new things when I was off duty, and more importantly, I was taking action. During the day time when I was off shift, I was learning and expanding my knowledge base. In the night time when I was on shift, I was arresting drunks, handling domestics, making traffic stops, conducting civil standbys, serving papers, getting into hot pursuits, assisting in search warrant executions, and literally being on shift during an officer-involved shooting where your elementary school teacher's husband, has just been shot three times. I ended up driving his vehicle from the crime scene to the hospital, where he was airlifted. Thankfully, that same Deputy survived, and the assailant was neutralized. He had made a full recovery within a few months.

But just imagine what that was like. I was a new cop who had only been hired for four days and found himself being told to drive the patrol vehicle of his elementary school teacher's husband, who had just been shot three times, according to your Sergeant. Before you can even ask more about what happened, you are running out the door with a department full of Sheriff's Deputies without a clue of what to do. Mind you, this is the same person you remember showing up for career day and talking about the very job you would end up choosing later in life. So it was personal.

I remembered this same Deputy coming to a career day when I was just in Elementary school. Everyone revered him and admired him like he was an Angel or God-like, and here he was over a decade later - being airlifted to the hospital while I was the guy who later took his patrol vehicle back to his wife (my elementary school teacher) at the hospital where he was airlifted to.

I remember seeing the look in her eyes when I returned this Deputy's patrol vehicle to her. She was filled with fear, emotion, and distress, as any spouse would be when their loved one has been shot by a wanted Felon and C.S.C predator. I remember we didn't say much to each other, but I had told her, "Your husband is a hero. He's going to make it." My elementary school teacher, in tears, smiled and thanked me. That was the end of our dialogue as things were chaotic and moving at 100 mph, but I remember that I did make her smile and help lighten the weight of the situation, even if it was only for a few seconds. I remember knowing that this Deputy was going to make it. I remember having what felt like almost a psychic premonition and could see the future with this Deputy still in it. Gladly, I was later proven to be right. The Deputy returned in only a few months with full functionality in all areas where he was shot (arm, leg, and just below his bulletproof vest near his belly button). But now, let us continue the original subject of this chapter - financial literacy and planning for all scenarios that can put your pensions or investments at risk.

For me, I was always a bit different when it came to "saving money." Today, I don't believe in saving money. I believe in investing money and then reinvesting it. In doing so, I have steady cash flow coming in every month, rather than storing away every penny and relying on the seductive match of a 401k or rescindable pension plan. My personal ways that I believed in managing my money were much more risky than what financial advisors like Dave Ramsey would recommend. I learned that the best way to make money for retirement purposes was to buy businesses, invest in rental properties, and create your own tangible assets (my screenplays and this book, for example). I also invested in anything that solved a multi-trillion-dollar problem and anything that I felt would inevitably appreciate in value within the next decade. If you're going to invest, invest in appreciating assets and assets that are tangible, distressed, or real.

I invested in the famous cross-border payment transaction currency, XRP (Ripple Labs Inc.), wrote several different screenplays that I had planned (and still) plan on selling, raised money from my earned income as a police officer, and eventually, used that money to take out a loan for my first rental property that earned me $400 per month. The rental property was the golden ticket that provided me with my first stable source of cash flow and passive income.

It took me many months of losing money on that rental property, however, before I began making my money back on it. Later after scaling revenue from my real estate properties, I would eventually acquire someone else's business through private equity deals. These would be businesses that were in distress, so I could fix one minor thing in the business model and later enjoy the cash flow that would come with the buy. I played my cards so that even if I had lost my job as a police officer in a theoretical scenario, I would still be able to pay my bills and live comfortably without that job.

I found a way to make money work for me while I sleep, and to me, this was a critical goal to conquer for my own well-being and for my future. Investing was the only real way to make money in my eyes. Most people commonly rely on a 401k, a pension plan with a 2.5 multiplier, or a Roth IRA. These are all options if you are looking to save money and wait until you are over 50 years old or higher to take that money out (while still being taxed and penalized horrifically in most cases).

In this career, you will see things that will always stay in your memory, and you will see things people should never have to see. You may very well become burnt out after just a year of being around dead bodies, gangs, car accidents, traumatic events, shootings, drownings, overdoses, excited delirium, sex offenders, pedophiles, and robberies on a daily basis. You will eventually look for financial freedom to avoid getting spat on, cussed out, disrespected, beaten, shot at, stabbed, assassinated, and unappreciated. My point is you will likely seek retirement before you ever reach 20 years as a police officer, no matter how badly you think you want this career now. You still need to plan while you're young, and if you're not young, you need to consider such contingencies and whether or not you really want to become a police officer.

Weigh your pros and cons, and don't be afraid to admit to yourself that perhaps you simply may not want this career as badly as you thought. Do you want to be rich? Or do you want to be financially stable and solely a police officer? If you are looking to accomplish both, then it will require a methodical path of working your full-time job as an officer and a profitable side hustle that doesn't require too much work. Use the side hustle to raise money so you buy that first rental property as I did, and from there on, just keep on growing. You should strongly consider this question and find the answer at your earliest convenience.

Another important thing to consider, now that you have learned how the ultra-rich make their money, is whether or not you have good credit. If you want to build businesses while being a police officer, and if you ever want to get into real estate investing, then you will need to have at least a credit score of 680 or higher so you can get the best terms on conventional loans (home loans) or SBA loans (small business loans). Everything in America comes down to the banking and financial industries, so you have to always make sure you are doing whatever you can to get your credit score to 800 plus so you can effortlessly invest and get the easiest loans to pay back (and yes, without taking out loans, you will never become wealthy or be able to acquire assets).

That is another misconception police officers and the average person make when it comes to building wealth. 99% of people don't understand how to utilize and properly manage loans. Many believe that loans are bad and that you should always try to live debt free. This is false. Although it is very true that you should TRY to be debt free and never take out a loan, that is very difficult for the average person who has no money. That is why we have credit.

Credit is money for people who don't have money. If you use credit as a tool and a resource, then credit cards will be your best friend and will buy you anything you want in life if used in the creatively correct ways. It is also okay to be in debt AS LONG as you are good at paying your debts back. It really is that simple. If you are going to be an entrepreneur or business owner, then debt is your best friend, and you probably won't be able to scale without it. Debt can afford to build you that startup office that may cost you $10,000 to renovate/refurbish. Debt can afford you an $80,000 vehicle so long as the vehicle is under an LLC and listed under business expenses, where taxes can pass through the business owner and directly to the business. In such an instance, that $80,000 you spent as a business expense and took out a loan for is now deemed a tax write-off and free essentially. Because of a person's history of paying back their debt and raising their credit score to a high enough number of 760, for example, for at least four years - this person can easily get that $80,000 business vehicle written off tax-free.

This is why it is important that every police officer who seeks to become an entrepreneur read the book "Rich Dad Poor Dad", where the secrets of real estate investing, taxes, business, and entrepreneurialism are broken down into detail-oriented chapters, teaching readers specifically how to start and scale a business, as well as how to invest in real estate and other forms of appreciating assets. This is how I learned the ways of the wealthy, simply by reading that very book by Robert Kiyosaki. Remember this, if nothing else - if you don't read, then you will never lead. Be a reader so you can be a leader for humanity. On top of that, make sure you are, most importantly, taking action.

Chapter 8: The 3 Paths - It is Important to Know What is and isn't Important

Before you make the leap to become a police officer, you should also know the three fundamental options for which path is the best path to take. It is important to know what is and isn't important along your journey in not just becoming a cop but also becoming financially free and independent. You need to know that not all paths are focused on a career in Law Enforcement. You need to know that accurate information in your daily life will develop who you are as a person, professional, and prodigy. In this chapter, we will discuss the high importance of obtaining accurate information in order to successfully become a police officer and a winner in life.

We will discuss what to expect when being asked to take personality tests and psychological evaluations in order to get hired at any police department or Sheriff's Office. Accurate information is key, and you must be intentional and honest about everything if you ever seek to become a police officer or a winner in everyday life. Honor, wisdom, generosity, valor, and compassion are the virtues of not only the chivalrous but also the God-like. It is not blasphemy or selfish to want to be God-like. As stated in the Holy Bible, we are created in the image of God. Therefore, you should not be afraid to reach for the stars and aspire to be God-like.

You will shine amongst the valley of competitors without a struggle if you learn to carry yourself in this image.

Here are the three paths that you will one day have to choose from if you haven't had to choose this path already. If you have already chosen one of these paths, then I implore you to read further and analyze yourself from a new perspective, as the information you are about to learn is very, very important.

The three paths in life are as follows:

1. Go to college, get a degree, and work for someone else for a decent salary and a paycheck. Perhaps become a police officer.

2. Don't go to college. Find a craft to hone, and master it until you are your own boss. Become self-employed and become your own boss as soon as you graduate High School. This is the greatest way to become wealthy and financially independent early in life.

3. Join the military, fight for your country, retire in a timely manner, and live off of the benefits until something better comes along. Lastly, this option is the more risky option, but it can also help astronomically in your journey of becoming a police officer.

The three paths are very important to consider if you are still in your younger years and trying to figure out whether or not you would like to become a police officer. Option 1 is the route I ultimately took. This by no means implies that the route I chose was the correct route, nor is it the route that you should pursue. This was the route that I chose because it worked for me, based on my own personality and plan and based on my own goals at the current time.

As a college student-athlete and aspiring police officer, I hated that I had to go back to school and get myself into debt just to secure a lousy, worthless degree. I hated college, although I excelled in it with ease. But in order to become a police officer and in order to continue playing football and baseball, I knew that I had to obtain that four-year Bachelor's Degree from a private school. Mainly, this was because I had practically gotten a free ride. There was very little college debt that I had to pay off in the end.

However, looking back on it all, I might have chosen a Community College to obtain the basic Associate's Degree required to get into the police academy. If I had been willing to sacrifice playing football and baseball in college, I would have only needed my Associate's Degree. I could have saved both time and money. Despite this, I have no regrets. If I had chosen a different path, I might have never written this book, and I may have never become a police officer.

In the end, I was surrounded by Pre-Med students and Pre-Law students, all indoctrinated by highly liberal and Marxist curriculums taught at the college I attended. Although Olivet College was generally a Christian private school, it had the same issue as any University in America of being extremely far-left in its approach to education and politics.

College was, in many ways illuminating because it showed me how NOT to think and how you should NOT see the world. When college professors taught me never to ask questions, I was selfish and asked many of them, like a kid who constantly asks, "Why, why, why," this is how I always forced myself to be in college because the knowledge, and accurate information, is scarce in a society of censorship and silence.

When college told me to shoot for an internship, I was shooting for the stars and doing what I could to start my own business. I had gotten to meet Medal of Honor recipient James C. McCloughan, who was a former United States Army soldier and a Vietnam War veteran because I took the initiative to talk to him and ask questions when he was a keynote speaker during a seminar. McCloughan was approved for the Medal of Honor by President Barack Obama and granted the medal by former President Donald Trump, and I not only met him but got a picture with him.

The point of these examples is to prove that, in some fashion, utilizing the path you take in life and making the most of that path will, without failure, open doors you never thought accessible. Be bold and force yourself to be resourceful and enthusiastic. Be happy to network with VIP-level people you wouldn't normally get a network with. This will carry you so much further when you are eventually hoping to impress your superiors in a police oral board interview or in a room where money is on the line. This will carry you further in business, as well as in everyday life.

In the human struggle to become anything important, it is important to know what is important and what is not important. That is basic wisdom that will not only allow you a more fluent path to becoming a police officer but will also open the gates for millions to be made in your life later while saving valuable, irreplaceable time. Use it or lose it. Be smart and be enterprising. As a cop, you will need to be, and you will need to be a master at it.

When college tried to brainwash me into becoming a Socialist and Communist, I began to relish in Capitalism and the American Dream. Since I was a little kid, I learned early that you could never bet against America… not unless you want to get chewed up, spit out, stepped on, and eaten again for seconds by Uncle Sam. He will gladly wipe his mouth with the money that he lends you, so he can continue controlling you until you die… and, of course, while repossessing the assets you leave behind. Never bet against America, and most certainly, never bet against the American Dream. As Toby Kieth once said, "Justice will be served, and the battle will rage. This big dog will fight when you rattle his cage. You'll be sorry that you messed with the U.S.A. 'Cause we'll put a boot in your ass. It's the American way".

As a cop, I constantly would have to analyze situations and ask myself, "What is important, and what is not important in everything this person is saying?" You need the facts. You must know what, where, when, why, and how events occur, have occurred, and could occur in the future. Information is important, and it is a catalyst for generating wealth and results in any and all endeavors. You must get good at placing events in chronological order, have a good memory, and be quick on your feet. Your prudence must be trustworthy and solid. You have to be physically able to do the job and mentally able to do it. Organizing your information and thoughts properly correlates with making swift and steady decisions on the fly. You have to be able to multitask and act when called upon. You have to be okay with making very little money for it. So when you choose which path you want to take, be sure you are ready if you seek the path of Law Enforcement.

When you are old and grey, you will be set in your ways, and it will be too late to go back in time to change the past. So be sure to know what is important and not important in life. That goes especially for which path you are going to take when deciding between these three paths. Part of this means being able to discern and identify who you are as a person and what you're likely to do when you're challenged with the option of going to college, becoming an entrepreneur, or choosing the military. Of course, there are other options for careers, but typically from my experience, most people that I have graduated with either chose the route of going to the military, college, or self-employment.

Everyone is different based on their long-term goals and personality. Granted, I don't believe the Meyers-Briggs is an accurate standard for career determination, intelligence quotient, or accurate personality classification. Every test is speculative in nature and has reasons for being accurate and inaccurate. What I do find useful with the Meyers-Briggs

Personality test, the DISC test, or Dark Triad tests, for instance, is that one can definitely help to learn what kind of thinker they are. You can learn what kind of lifestyle you envelope yourself in and possibly learn more about yourself by taking the tests I mentioned, honestly.

Before being hired into my first Sheriff's Department, I had to complete a psychological evaluation, with three other tests at the end of the evaluation. These three tests were the Meyers-Briggs Personality test, the Minnesota Multiphasic Personality Inventory test, and the DISC test. The MMPI test historically has been used as a psychological test that assesses personality traits and psychopathology. It is primarily intended to test people who are suspected of having mental health or other clinical issues. This is critical information and important information for any who seek to become Law Enforcement officers in the future. One should take these tests and study them before considering a position in the police academy, so one can learn how to pass them with ease. This is exactly what I did.

I researched that in most police agencies regarding psychological evaluations; it was common that you would have to take the same three tests I mentioned - the Meyers-Briggs Personality test, the Minnesota Multiphasic Personality Inventory test, the DISC test, and several other tests that I have taken the liberty to list below.

Psychological evaluations in Michigan may include a variety of tests and assessment tools depending on the purpose of the evaluation and the specific needs of the individual being evaluated. However, some commonly used tests in psychological evaluations, and the tests that took, include:

1. Intelligence Tests: The Wechsler Adult Intelligence Scale (WAIS) is used to measure an individual's cognitive abilities, including verbal comprehension, perceptual reasoning, working memory, and processing speed.

2. Personality Tests: These tests, such as the Minnesota Multiphasic Personality Inventory (MMPI) or the Millon Clinical Multiaxial Inventory (MCMI), are used to assess an individual's personality traits, emotional functioning, and mental health symptoms.

3. Projective Tests: The Rorschach Inkblot Test or the Thematic Apperception Test (TAT) are used to assess an individual's unconscious thoughts, emotions, and conflicts by asking them to respond to ambiguous stimuli.

4. Neuropsychological tests: These tests, such as the Wisconsin Card Sorting Test (WCST) or the Stroop Test, are used to assess an individual's cognitive functioning, attention, memory, and executive functioning.

5. Achievement tests: These tests, such as the Wide Range Achievement Test (WRAT) or the Woodcock-Johnson Tests of Achievement, are used to assess an individual's academic abilities, including reading, writing, and math skills.

Overall, the specific tests used in a psychological evaluation in Michigan will depend on the individual being evaluated and the purpose of the evaluation and will be selected by the licensed psychologist conducting the evaluations. Depending on which psychological examination you attend, these are key pieces of information to note in order to properly prepare yourself for what can be a highly intimidating procedure.

It could have been a very stressful thing to take these tests and not know how I performed on them. Thankfully, I studied the tests weeks before my psychological evaluation was scheduled, and when it came time to take the tests in the formal psychological evaluation, I nailed them without struggle and looked good in a suit while doing it.

Information is important because if I had never researched which tests to study for, I could have potentially failed simply by being TOO honest and forthright, not knowing how exactly the test was scored. Although I had already known that I was mentally strong enough to become a police officer, it concerned me that any fair-minded person who answered questions in a deceptive or unsure manner by accident could have been written off and swept away from a career in Law Enforcement. Accurate information is important, and it is also important when it comes to choosing a path in life.

We all have certain personality types, and because of this, some career paths may be more suitable for specific personality types. For example, the ENTJ (Extraverted, Intuitive, Thinking, Judging), known as "the Commander", is my personality type along with an INTJ, depending on my mood I'm in. Both ENTJ and INTJ personality types allegedly tend to gravitate towards careers as police officers, CEOs, engineers, politicians, managers, producers, or developers. I have often scored as both the INTJ, usually fluctuating from one to another each time I take the test. I have also scored as an INFJ personality type, as well as the ENTP personality type from time to time. These scores often change, and for this reason, I have felt that these tests are not to be trusted as solid, fool proof mechanisms for declaring any one particular personality type. This is because as human beings, we have ever changing personality types based on our life circumstances, changes in belief, lifestyle habits, and perspectives. The ENTJ and INTJ, which I have most often scored as, are known as "Shapers" or "Architects" in the modern day world. There are 16 personality types, and many are compatible for different career paths. They are as follows:

1. ISTJ (Introverted, Sensing, Thinking, Judging): This personality type is practical, logical, and organized. They are responsible, dependable, and follow the rules. The "Logistician" personality type.
2. ISFJ (Introverted, Sensing, Feeling, Judging): ISFJs are warm, caring, and loyal. They are detail-oriented and enjoy helping others. They are "The Nurturer" on the MBPT.
3. INFJ (Introverted, Intuitive, Feeling, Judging): This personality type is insightful, empathetic, and creative. They have a strong sense of purpose and enjoy helping others. They are "The Advocates" or "Idealists". This is the rarest personality type of the 16 Meyers-Briggs Personality Test.
4. INTJ (Introverted, Intuitive, Thinking, Judging): INTJs are strategic, analytical, and independent. They are goal-oriented and enjoy solving complex problems. These personality types are known as "Architects." These are the third rare personality types.
5. ISTP (Introverted, Sensing, Thinking, Perceiving): This personality type is adventurous, logical, and practical. They are skilled at fixing things and enjoy hands-on work. They are "The Craftsmen" on the Personality Test.

6. ISFP (Introverted, Sensing, Feeling, Perceiving): ISFPs are sensitive, artistic, and gentle. They enjoy expressing themselves through creative pursuits. Known as "The Artist."

7. INFP (Introverted, Intuitive, Feeling, Perceiving): This personality type is idealistic, empathetic, and creative. They are deeply committed to their values and enjoy helping others. These are known as "The Mediators."

8. INTP (Introverted, Intuitive, Thinking, Perceiving): INTPs are analytical, curious, and logical. They enjoy exploring new ideas and solving complex problems. These are identified as "The Scientists."

9. ESTP (Extraverted, Sensing, Thinking, Perceiving): This personality type is energetic, confident, and action-oriented. They are skilled at adapting to new situations and enjoy taking risks. These characters are commonly known as "The Entrepreneur" personality type.

10. ESFP (Extraverted, Sensing, Feeling, Perceiving): ESFPs are outgoing, enthusiastic, and fun-loving. They enjoy socializing and entertaining others. Known as "The Entertainer" personality type.

11. ENFP (Extraverted, Intuitive, Feeling, Perceiving): This personality type is enthusiastic, imaginative,

and empathetic. They enjoy exploring new ideas and possibilities. They are known as "The Champion."

12. ENTP (Extraverted, Intuitive, Thinking, Perceiving): ENTPs are creative, curious, and innovative. They enjoy debating ideas and exploring new concepts. They are known as "The Debater."

13. ESTJ (Extraverted, Sensing, Thinking, Judging): This personality type is practical, organized, and decisive. They are natural leaders and enjoy taking charge. Identified as "The Director" or "Supervisor."

14. ESFJ (Extraverted, Sensing, Feeling, Judging): ESFJs are warm, friendly, and helpful. They are good at organizing and supporting others. Commonly known as "The Caregiver."

15. ENFJ (Extraverted, Intuitive, Feeling, Judging): This personality type is charismatic, empathetic, and persuasive. They enjoy leading and inspiring others. These are known as "The Mentor" or "Protagonist."

16. ENTJ (Extraverted, Intuitive, Thinking, Judging): ENTJs are ambitious, strategic, and assertive. They enjoy organizing and leading others towards achieving their goals. They are the second-rarest personality type, known as "The Commanders."

The DISC assessment is very similar, as it assesses your behavioral patterns, essentially showing behavioral characteristics of either Dominant, Influence, Steadiness,

Compliance or a combination thereof. My score for the DISC assessment is a high D. I have often scored a high DI from time to time.

The validity of the DISC test has been supported by research, indicating that it is a reliable and valid tool for assessing an individual's behavioral tendencies. This is why it is commonly used in psychological evaluations. I remember taking this test when I was in the room taking my tests. However, it's important to note that the DISC test is not designed to diagnose mental health disorders and should not be used as a substitute for professional clinical assessment.

In Michigan, the DISC test may be used in a variety of settings, including career development, employee selection, team building, and personal growth. Many employers use the DISC test as a part of their hiring process to help identify candidates who are a good fit for the job and the company culture. In addition, the DISC test can be used to help individuals gain a better understanding of their own behavioral style and how they can work more effectively with others.

Overall, the DISC test is a valuable tool for assessing an individual's behavioral style and preferences and can be used in a variety of settings to support personal and professional growth. However, it is important to use the test in conjunction with other assessment tools and professional clinical assessment when necessary.

Other tests that I have found very useful in identifying unique personality traits and characteristics, but did not remember taking in my psychological evaluations, were the Enneagram and H.E.X.A.C.O (Honesty, Emotionality, Extraversion, Agreeableness, Conscientiousness, and Openness), personality tests. I have often scored as a Type Eight for the Enneagram. For the H.E.X.A.C.O, I often score high on the Openness, Conscientiousness, and Extraversion scales. There are many other psychological tests available on the internet that can help define your own personality traits and characteristics in your search for finding fitting career paths, romantic partners, cultural adaptability levels, intelligence quotients, and other facets of everyday life.

The reason I wrote this chapter was to further educate you on the process of not just how to become a police officer and how to pass the prerequisite psychological examination but also how to choose the right path in life by using accurate information and resources to do so.

Accurate information and choosing the correct path is something very critical when you are driving hot to a barricaded gunman or planning your retirement strategy. It is important when you are choosing the right person to marry or the right business to start. Remember - In the human struggle to become anything important, it is important to know what is important and what is not important. Choose your path based on the comparisons of risk versus reward and opportunity versus cost. Be wise in the path you choose, take the path less traveled, and take the path that will create generational happiness and satisfaction. Knowing what is and isn't important is very important.

PART II: The Police Academy, Getting Hired, and Keeping the Job

Chapter 9: The Police Academy

The Beginning…

Welcome to Part II of this book, where I talk about my experiences in the police academy and the catalyst for what brought me to where I am today. If you have made it this far into the book, then you are truly dedicated to becoming a police officer. If you skipped forward to this part in the book, then I suggest going back and reading Part I when you are ready, as it will help explain my purpose in writing this book, as well as some basic questions you will need to ask yourself before considering a career in Law Enforcement.

I have already discussed the high importance of meeting all necessary requirements before moving further to becoming a police officer, such as deciding what career path you should take and passing the background check and psychological exam, for example. Part II of this book will be more Law Enforcement oriented, focused on the in-depth details of getting through the police academy, graduating, getting hired, and keeping the job. I will discuss many of my own failures and downfalls, as well as my successes and how I chose to solve and evolve throughout moments of adversity in my journey to becoming a police officer.

I remember the day I received an email from my police academy director stating that I had been accepted into the police academy. This was after I had already passed a background check, an English/grammar pre-test required by the state of Michigan, a drug test, and a physical fitness test also required by the state. A week before I had been accepted into the police academy, I was completing the last step in the process of getting accepted, which was the oral board interview. I was wearing my best suit with my hair spiked, clean shaven, clean cut, clothes pressed, and awaiting one of the most nerve-wracking milestones in my life - the police academy oral board interview.

This was during the COVID-19 pandemic, so it was required that all candidates interviewing were to wear a face mask during the course of my oral board interview that day.

Quite frankly, I thought this to be moronic and unnecessary, as today's data has come to prove. I remember hating that I was forced to wear a face mask that day. I wasn't able to show my face, smile, or show my emotions, which I knew could help me stand out in my interview. The smile you put on your face is a magnet of influence and attraction by design, so why not smile more? To me, not getting to use my face to my advantage felt detrimental to my chances of success. I wanted to show who I was. But I remembered that the eyes were the window to the soul. I knew they would be able to see my eyes, so I made sure to use this to my advantage.

I had to adapt and endure and reverse my way of thinking. I made sure anything visible during the interview was pristine and well groomed, clean pressed, with not a single hair or speck out of place. I made sure my hair looked clean-cut and well-groomed. I made sure my suit was appropriately boring and nice but not too distracting to the eyes of the audience. If I could not use my smile to draw attraction and interest, I would use my transparency, honesty, and integrity. I would use my sense of humor, and appeal to the interests of my interviewers (the director and two other instructors). I would show interest in their own journeys and their own personal lives in order to connect and develop rapport. This is the art of communication and how you should approach your interview.

If this didn't work, I had my perfect totem to secure my position in the police academy, which was a drawing I had made in a Kindergarten class stating, "I am lovable because I like to save people." This was a picture I had made when I was little, showing me saving someone who was stuck in a jungle gym. In the picture, I was wearing a police uniform. I had kept that picture for years, and I used it for many of my Law Enforcement interviews. I would end every interview with a presentation of the drawing and say, "I know that everyone going into Law Enforcement probably says that they have always wanted to be a police officer since they were five years old, but I have the proof." At this point, I would display the drawing and close the deal. My instructors loved it because it was honest but also original, genuine, and legitimate proof that I have always wanted to become a police officer at some point in my life.

I remember sitting alone in the cafeteria and being the first one there on interview day. My knee bounced rapidly, and I remember hardly being able to breathe. I had butterflies and what felt like hives forming from the stress. Simultaneously, I enjoyed the rush, and I knew that I was going to crush the interview. I was fully prepared and ready for any questions my future instructors were going to ask. I practiced my responses in a mirror again and again until I was more than ready for showtime.

It was intimidating. I was in a room of people who were just as ambitious and like-minded as me. I was going up against classmates who were just turning 21 out of the Explorer's program, not even old enough to drink yet, but still had more Law Enforcement experience than me. I was just a 22-year-old college student-athlete, with only two internships with the Sheriff's Department I later got hired at. That was the only hands-on experience I had in Law Enforcement besides a vocational public safety class I had taken in high school. College was primarily academic in terms of learning the foundations of the Criminal Justice system. The textbook we read was the same textbook that we read in the academy. That was about the only advantage I had in terms of hands-on experience.

In the police academy, I was going up against mothers and fathers, and in one instance, even a Grandma who was able to run 5 miles without issue. These were all people who looked like they were my age, even though they were often twice my age in both academies I graduated from. Before my classmates made a choice to become police officers, many of them were usually dispatchers, correctional officers, and security officers before finding their way to the police academy. Some had jobs working with the Department of Defense, some had combat experience in the military with top-secret clearance, and some were nurses and bartenders before they became police officers and academy candidates. Some were musicians, and one kid was even a farmer who had moved to Michigan from Alabama to pursue the path of Law Enforcement. My classmates in both academies came from all different walks of life, and when you find yourself in the police academy, you will notice the same.

The next step, after making it through the interviewing stage and finally receiving the acceptance letter or email, is orientation day. Orientation day consists of a 2-hour class providing you with your assigned seats, expectations for day #1 of the police academy, as well as distribution of uniforms and textbooks. Everything is a test. From the very moment you enter the classroom, you are being judged on your response to pressure and criticism. You are being evaluated from the very moment you submit your application.

After orientation day came day #1, which was about a week after the orientation day for both of my academics. Day #1 will be different at every academy. From state to state, county to county, academy to academy, there will be unique structures for how the academy will be organized, so my experience may vary in contrast to yours. My police academy was a paramilitary academy, so everything was high intensity all the time and very strict on rules and appearance.

In my police academy, day #1 consisted of being screamed at and overwhelmed with information and textbooks. We were instructed to line up against the wall in the gymnasium in number order and stand at rest or attention. After minutes of everyone remaining silent, suddenly, a Michigan State Trooper, County Sheriff's Deputy, and City Police Officer marched into the gymnasium shouting expletives at us. We were all terrified, and it was absolute chaos. For me, I had expected it and knew that the first day was more about surviving the day and pushing through the pressure and fear. Day #1 was a test of how badly you really wanted to become a police officer. In both police academies that I attended, there was one quitter in a class of 26 cadets. In many academies, there will always be at least one quitter.

Depending on the school and the training curriculum, there can be a wide range in the attrition (dropout) rate in police academies. However, it happens frequently for some cadets to drop out of the academy training program due to a lack of motivation or desire to continue pursuing the career.

The physical and mental strains of the training, difficulties with academic work, and personal or family problems can all cause cadets to leave the academy. It's challenging to provide a precise figure because it varies based on the area, academy, and recruitment class. If I had to guess, across America, I would estimate that at least 5-20% will eventually drop on request from their chosen academies.

If your tie was not plain black, with a clip-on, and looking exactly like everyone else's, you were scorned and ridiculed for your insolence and failure to follow instructions with attention to detail. If your boots were not polished with a shine and a perfect gig line at the belt, with a correctly pressed uniform, then you would be singled out (like I was, as much as I hate to admit) and be issued a demerit. I received about ten demerits in each police academy, as I was always a rule breaker and liked to have a little too much fun. Same as High School. I would be lying if I told you I was at the front of the class and the perfect cadet. I was anything but.

I was more or so in the back of the class. I was a C student in my first academy and a B student in my second academy. I always sucked at taking tests. My homework assignments would be finished and done properly, but my quizzes and exams would often score low. Throughout my first academy, I was a C student and had the second to lowest G.P.A. Throughout my second academy, I was a B student who was right in the middle of the class in terms of G.P.A. I should have been an A student considering the fact that I had already graduated from the previous academy, knowing exactly what to expect on each exam, so all of the material was fresh in my mind. Still - even with that advantage, I was only a B student at best. If I'm being honest, that was more or so because I may have had too much fun in the academy than I should've. To me, life is all about fun and games, mainly because life is just that - a game.

Needless to say, I was never going to stand a chance at getting hired at the higher paying departments like Sterling Heights or Rochester Police Department. I was a slacker in terms of grade point average if I had to categorize myself amongst the flock while I was in the police academy. I was one of the daydreamers who would look out the window in class, fill my notes with random doodle drawings, bounce my knee, and fall asleep on and off throughout the classroom portion of the police academy. I was never great in a classroom environment because I've never been good at being stagnant and sedentary. I love to move fast, and I love to get things done. I have always been industrious and action-based.

I learned to become a good listener only after becoming a police officer after growing in experience and learning to speak with confidence and authority while focusing on what the other person was saying in this process... in other words

- multitasking. This skill is so important and one that is essential. You must become great at not only listening but multitasking and becoming assertive. You must be assertive in both your verbal tone and your physical presence. You must get good at taking control over situations while listening to everything being said in the background while simultaneously thinking of your next move and how you will approach incoming situations. Your mind needs to move fast, and it needs to move with sound judgment. This is the same in not only Law Enforcement and everyday life but especially business, being an entrepreneur, and life.

You have to be fast, and you have to move quickly. Everyone is slow, like molasses. You have to get good at thinking on your feet quickly, and making decisions, all while absorbing the information being transmitted around you. Your neurons should be firing every second of the day, constantly working. You are constantly transmitting valuable and priceless information that could potentially save someone's life, including your own. This is why you must learn to think fast and move fast - both in Law Enforcement and when you are starting any kind of business. Learn to multitask and make decisions both logically and reasonably, but most importantly - learn to make them quickly. This will save you valuable time, money, and energy. This will give you a tremendous competitive edge over those who are slow, lazy, and indecisive.

Learning to focus on the conversation at hand while simultaneously focusing on the millions of moving parts happening around me was a skill that took time to master, and it is a skill that you can never stop learning. It was hard to do these things and take control over the situations I faced on the job until I knew how to do my job and do it well - which meant listening and listening well. Before learning how to be a good police officer, I did not know how to listen well because I was focused on the millions of moving parts around me, as mentioned before. When I learned the job and became comfortable with how to approach specific calls, I became more confident and relaxed - which later allowed me to listen and, eventually, listen well.

For example, I learned to listen to my radio while I was simultaneously listening to someone speak, all while scanning the room around me for immediate threats and potential escape routes. I learned how to listen to the radio, drive at dangerously high speeds to emergency calls (safely), and work the different sirens at the same time, all while managing to take direction from a G.P.S and Field Training Officer while still focusing on incoming traffic and pedestrians in close proximity around me. These are the necessary skills needed in any properly functioning police officer or high-efficiency individual. Speed and the ability to multitask are critical to your survival in anything.

In school, you are taught to be soft and slow. You are taught to never make mistakes and are indoctrinated to become afraid of making decisions. You are especially discouraged from making decisions quickly, for that matter. This is why 99% fail. You have been brainwashed into believing that taking your time and not making mistakes will lead you to success, but that is false. You need to be a quick, decisive thinker and a relentless action-taker. You need to be quick-brained and fast-moving, as the universe is always operating at such speed.

Getting good at overcoming tunnel vision taught me how to listen and listen well. You must learn to listen and listen well in order to achieve any desired output from your audience. How good are you at listening? Can you remember the most previous conversation you had, who it was with, and what the summary of the conversation was? Are you good at remembering names, dates, times, colors, shapes, and numbers? These are all traits that any police officer must master. Learn to master not only your listening skills but your memory skills as well. Memory is one with listening.

In the police academy, every day is Hell. It is fun, but it is long, strenuous, tiring, and mentally and physically draining. It is tough, no doubt about it. At least, that was the case in the academy that I attended. I went to a paramilitary academy that was all about "Yes Sir, No Sir, or Yes ma'am, or no ma'am." It was obvious that you would not speak unless spoken to. We would march everywhere we went and spoke with a standard of respect, authority, and compliance. I would often get in trouble because I was terrible at the compliance part. I was always getting into trouble. In both academies that I graduated from, I had just about the same amount of demerits in each class, amounting to about 10 in each academy.

The police academy I attended was broken up into sections. The first section was seven weeks of classroom-based curriculum studying the "Criminal Law and Procedures" textbook. After the first two weeks, PT begins. After week 3, firearms qualification begins. After the firearms qualifications, subject control begins. Just about the same time that subject control starts, you go to Emergency Vehicle Operations. Following this, First Aid begins. After you've passed your exams for First Aid, you get pepper sprayed, and in some academies, even taser certified.

Each police academy is different. You will learn different tactical skill sets based on the different academies you attend. For instance, in some police academies, you may learn Brazilian Jiu-Jitsu as your Subject Control fighting style. In other academies, you may learn Krav Maga or Systema. In some police academies, you may qualify with different firearms. I qualified with the Glock 17 handgun and Remington .870 pump-action Shotgun. We were familiarized with the AR-15. Some cadets who were sponsored by their respective departments were required to use a certain calibre bullet. Every academy and every department is a bit different and unique in its own way.

The most challenging part of the academy was getting up and showing up every day, knowing that you were going to be worked until you had nothing left in the tank. I remember that my police academy was about a 40-minute drive from my house. Fortunately, unlike many academies, our academy didn't make us remain at the training facility every day. However, I hated getting up at 5:00 am every morning and driving to the academy that was about 40 minutes away - especially in my first academy, when it was freezing cold and miserable Michigan weather all around.

I remember being half awake, sore, and mentally exhausted on my way to the police academy every morning. You would think I was drunk at the wheel if you were behind me because I was always struggling to stay awake and not fall into a deep sleep. I know… I should've gotten up earlier, eaten a better breakfast, and drank a coffee before I left. You got me. Guilty as charged. However, I can't say that I never tried to do all of those things. The truth is, no matter how early you get up, no matter how much coffee you drank, and what kind of breakfast you ate, you'd still be falling asleep uncontrollably simply when considering how hard you were pushing your body and mind in the police academy.

Remember - I graduated from two consecutive academies and was never sponsored by a department, so I was never even getting paid for completing twice the amount of training (taking a year of my life away). I remember showing up to the training center at 7:00 am in full PT gear, ready to kick off the day with a 1-mile warm-up run, doing as many push-ups and sit-ups that you could do in 60 seconds while then having to do wall jumps and then finally whatever the workout for the day would be. Then, you'd still be running a few more miles after that, doing swimming evolutions, and questioning whether or not it's worth it to be a cop. At some point, almost everyone asks the question, "Is this really even worth it"?

I remember the first day of PT was obviously getting to know who our instructor would be. I had the same instructor in both academies. The typical workouts that we did in the academy consisted mostly of running about 2-5 miles a day, pushing cop cars, doing Indian runs, too many burpees, and preparation for the police academy's state-mandated PT exam. We never did much weight training, of course, which is where I would've excelled, as I was in 2nd and 3rd place in my High School state championship meets.

Everything in my academy was all cardio-based workouts. The worst part was my academy required all cadets to wear a face mask at all times throughout the day in both academies due to the Covid-19 pandemic (which was highly politicized and propagated). Imagine running 2-5 miles every day and not being able to take your mask off unless you were going outside. In the winter academy (the first academy I graduated from), this was almost never the case. We would do our PT inside in the hot gymnasium, wearing a face covering, sucking the mask in so badly that we could hardly breathe at all. It sucked more than anything I can remember, having to comply with such senseless mandates.

The Police Academy Covid Dilemma

I am fortunate that we were never required to receive the Covid injection as a prerequisite for getting accepted into the academy or graduating because I, personally, would have never complied with such draconian rules. If that had been the case, I would have never graduated from the police academy or written this book simply because I would have never taken that vaccine. I don't care what anyone else thinks about the vaccine, as everyone has a choice to come to their own conclusions about the vaccine, but I personally was always against what seemed to be a politically driven operation by the government to control and test compliance of the masses. Why would I have gotten the vaccine in that case? All because the government told me to? Get real. I'm a cop, and I swore an oath to honor the Constitution - not violate it and enforce tyrannical sanctions on other human beings - especially those who were trying to serve their country and become police officers.

I was able to discern a truth from a lie, and much of the events we observed in the Covid times were just that - lies and fiction. All for the political purposes of the ruling elites. Plus, all of the Covid hysteria was highly driven by malice, and ill will, with a touch of illegal and experimental trials, as we have learned through extensive research studies and patients who are permanently affected by the Covid injections today. Look at the Tuskegee Experiment, for example.

Although there are many of you who will disagree, and many cops who will disagree with me, the fact is - the world was tricked and persuaded by fear and propaganda for the purposes of depopulation, and it is a truth they don't want you to know. Many were not able to tell that it was a fraud, a plan, and a well-orchestrated symphony to control the minds of the masses and divide the world - all for population control and the financial incentive of the globalist ruling class. I knew this because I had met and had long conversations with individuals who were in the F.B.I. and C.I.A. They were some of my very own mentors during my time in college, working to get my Criminal Justice Degree. I was also very close with top Law Enforcement Officers and Sheriffs' Deputies (not at the department I worked for) who were members of the G.H.O.S.T unit and also awake to objectives being forwarded by local politicians just in the state I was working in. Out of respect and for the safety of these individuals, I will keep their names classified, as I have not received their permission to speak about them in this book.

I was not going to be one of the people who aided and embedded the politicians and bureaucrats in Washington who were used by the CIA as mindless puppets to divert the public from the true, accurate, well-debated, well-known information learned about the infectious disease. I would rather die on my feet than live on my knees. I felt it important to talk openly about my thoughts on this matter, as I am aware of how the world operates behind closed doors. Although I am only just a police officer, I am still friends with people who know much more than me and people who work in the darkest parts of today's world. Unfortunately, the world is not all sunshine and rainbows, as Rocky Balboa once said. It is a dangerous place where evil most certainly lurks in every space around you. If you are going to be a police officer, I do advise that you prepare to learn things you never thought possible. Now that I have fully warned you and disclosed this information regarding government involvement in the world or current events let us continue with the information you bought this book for. The police academy.

The Day in the Life of a Cadet

PT was easily what I did not miss about the police academy, especially since I was very poor at preparing myself for the academy. Although I was still in decent shape going into both the police academies I graduated from, I was still not in good enough shape. Yet, there were 45-year-olds, literally Grandparents, some of them, and still kicking my ass every time we would do a 2-5 mile run. It was like I was surrounded by a bunch of total badasses who were born perfectionists, more than I already was. It truly sucked to be this All-State football player, baseball player, and powerlifter and still be trailing behind a wolf den of competitors just as skilled, focused, and as capable as me, if not more. There was a lot of humility, but I learned that there is always a bigger bear, always a stronger competitor, and always a faster runner. I learned to be okay with competing with those who were at the same level or higher, and I learned to be okay with it. At the end of the day, you should always be competing with others who will force you to elevate and increase your work ethic, so you reach higher and higher levels of success. You are who you hang with, as we discussed earlier in this book.

After PT was over at 7:30, we would have to shower as fast as possible, change into our Class A uniforms (or Class Bs), and would always start with a roll call and daily inspection at 0800 sharp. If it was an all-classroom day, then you would be wearing the ugly, plain, tan uniforms that were usually too big or too hot to wear all day. If you were wearing the Class Bs, you would be wearing a dark blue academy t-shirt over your bullet proof vest. You would always have your gear belt on and tactical pants, with the boots spit-shined.

If, for some reason, you were like me in the academy, where your boots were constantly scuffed, sometimes forgetting your nametag, or not having my gig line perfect - then you would be issued a demerit or, if you were lucky, asked to do 25-50 pushups. Again, I got 10 of these demerits in both academies that I attended. I find myself to be blessed that I did make it through it all and that God saw the potential in me. I was nearly kicked out of the police academy a few times simply because I had gotten so many demerits and merely refused to wear the ridiculous face masks all day, every day. My rebellious nature nearly leads to my downfall as an aspiring police officer, so I strongly advise you - don't be like me in those regards.

Remember, this was all during the Covid-19 pandemic, so as you could imagine, a bunch of cops in the same building, of course, went right along with the rules made by the academy's Board of Administrators. I was always in trouble and getting talked to by my Director, who, quite frankly, was very patient with me and is the sole reason I was able to become a police officer. If it wasn't for him, I would have found myself either not being able to afford the second academy I graduated from or booted from it based on the number of demerits I had alone.

Yes, I was never the perfect cadet, and I made many, many, many mistakes along the way, but regardless, I am proud to have made it through the storm. The amount of people I have been able to help because of the badge I earned has been worth every single grueling morning of Hell and exhaustion. Although the pay is not what it should be as a police officer, it was never about the money for me. Despite my lifelong entrepreneurial spirit, I became a cop because I believed that serving my community and country was far more important than any dollar value I could make at another time in my life. I have no regrets about becoming a police officer, as it is bigger and more important than any title, net worth, or reputation. It is all about people and making the world a better place to the greatest extent possible.

Learning the Laws of the Land

In the first seven weeks, much of our time was primarily based on learning the laws and procedures of Michigan. Mainly focusing strongly on the Constitutional Amendments and learning the in-depth laws attached to each Amendment. Although every Amendment created is equally important, the First Amendment (Freedom to express speech, ideas, and religion), Second Amendment (the right to keep and bear arms), Fourth (protection against unreasonable search and seizures), Fifth (right to remain silent and not incriminate oneself), Sixth Amendment (right to legal representation when accused of a crime), Eighth (right to Due Process), and Thirteenth Amendments (right to a speedy trial) were the most critical Amendments that I remember our Attorney teaching us in the police academy.

Every Monday, you would meet in the computer lab to take a 100-question quiz summarizing everything the attorney had taught you about the complexities of the laws mended by the Supreme Court and by the state of Michigan.

For example, some of the most important things we had to learn were the detailed confounds of the 4th Amendment in the Constitution. I remember how confusing it was to finally understand the difference between plain view and open view.

Plain view can be used to justify the collection of evidence (drugs, weapons, or other elements of a crime) when an officer is inside of a home or confined space, discovering the evidence when it is uncovered or not hidden from sight. This would then cancel the need for a search warrant because the item is already in plain sight or plain view. For instance, if an officer is speaking with an individual in their home and they observe there to be a bag of cocaine sitting on the table, unhidden from a reasonable person's eye, then that would be an example of plain view.

Open view is merely the same, only it is the discovery of evidence when the officer is looking into a confined space from the outside, also discovering the evidence unhidden and in open view of the officer. At least, this is how I was taught the law. If an officer is driving behind a vehicle, for example, and observes what appears to be an AK47 sitting in the rear view windshield, unhidden and able to be seen by anyone, then this would be an example of open view.

Plain View and Open View were extremely important concepts to learn, and many of us took a long time to understand the difference between the two completely. I discerned this in both of my academies. This was only one subject area out of many that were very confusing and took a lot of studying.

The definition of the Fourth Amendment is "the people to be secure in their persons, houses, papers, and effects, against unreasonable searches and seizures. It is a Constitutional right that shall not be violated, and no warrants shall issue but upon probable cause, supported by Oath or affirmation, and particularly describing the place to be searched and the persons or things to be seized." The Fourth Amendment was one of the most prominent things taught to us in the police academy, as the Fourth Amendment secures a person's right to privacy. It is more a human right in many aspects of the law, and that is why it is so important.

Much of those first seven weeks were spent learning similar laws alike to this, such as The Exclusionary Rule and The Fruit of the Poisonous Tree Doctrine. We learned much about the critical case law related to the First, Second, Fourth, Fifth, Sixth, Eighth, and Thirteenth Amendments. An example of the case law I remember being drilled on was Miranda v. Arizona (the right to remain silent), which was a Supreme Court Case allowing the exercising of a person's Fifth Amendment (the right to not incriminate oneself). I remember learning about Tennessee v. Gardner (deadly force), Graham v. Connor and Butler v. Detroit (use of reasonable force), Floyd v. Chauvin (misuse of combat restraints and officer intervention), Giglio v. United States (protection against impeachment for government employees), and Pennsylvania v. Mimms (right to order a person out of a vehicle). There were many, many other case laws that I remember studying in the academy, but those were the most focused areas of study.

Fun & Guns

The first seven weeks were essentially classroom material for the listed subjects. On week 7, we were required to pass the legal exam with at least a 70% in under two attempts, or else we would be eliminated from moving forward in the academy. Every week you would take a 100-question exam, and your score would generally contribute to your ranking in the class or G.P.A. I remember my first time going through the academy, and I had failed the legal exam by one question. I remember being scared shitless that I was not going to move on and conquer my dreams of becoming a police officer, but fortunately, I was able to pass that legal exam on the second attempt with a 73% exactly (again - I was never a great test taker). Of course, however, I had later failed the state exam twice in my first police academy after graduating, requiring me to graduate AGAIN from the ENTIRE academy a second time. I always wonder, "Where would I be today if I quit and never tried again"?

At about week #3, firearms training began. At this point, we no longer would have to wear those hideous, Godforsaken tan uniforms that were thick, hot, plain, and too baggy. Now, we would finally get to wear our Class B's, which consisted of tactical pants, your gear belt, an academy embroidered t-shirt that you would wear over your bullet proof vest, and a baseball cap. I remember they were way better looking, cooler, less heavy, and far more comfortable than the tan uniforms.

Firearms training was intimidating for me because I never grew up learning about firearms or even being familiarized with them. I never had a dad to really teach me. I remember my dad wanting to teach me when I was younger but was never able to, as my mother was highly afraid of guns and advised against it. The most familiarity I ever had with firearms was when I would hang out with my redneck friends in High School and shoot skeet or sling a crossbow after school, which was not too often, but every now and then. I remember going shooting with my Step Grandfather and his cousin Pete who owned a gun shop in my hometown. I remember getting to shoot an AK74-U, a Glock 19, an AR-15, and a vintage M-14 Grant that was refurbished from World War II when I was there, and just like Jake Gyllenhaal from Jarhead, "I was hooked." Despite my lack of experience, I was always still a damn good shot.

When we started off with firearms in the academy, before we ever got into the range, we were briefed on the mechanisms of the weapons we would be firing (Glock 17,

Remington .870 Shotgun, and an AR-15). We took inventory and wrote down serial numbers; then, we would be trained on the proper ways to safely fire the weapons. Before ever getting to even pull the trigger, we were required to learn the 4 Firearms Cardinal Safety Rules and recite them 25 times (x50 times, including both academies I graduated from) as a homework assignment. Here was mine (don't mind the white out).

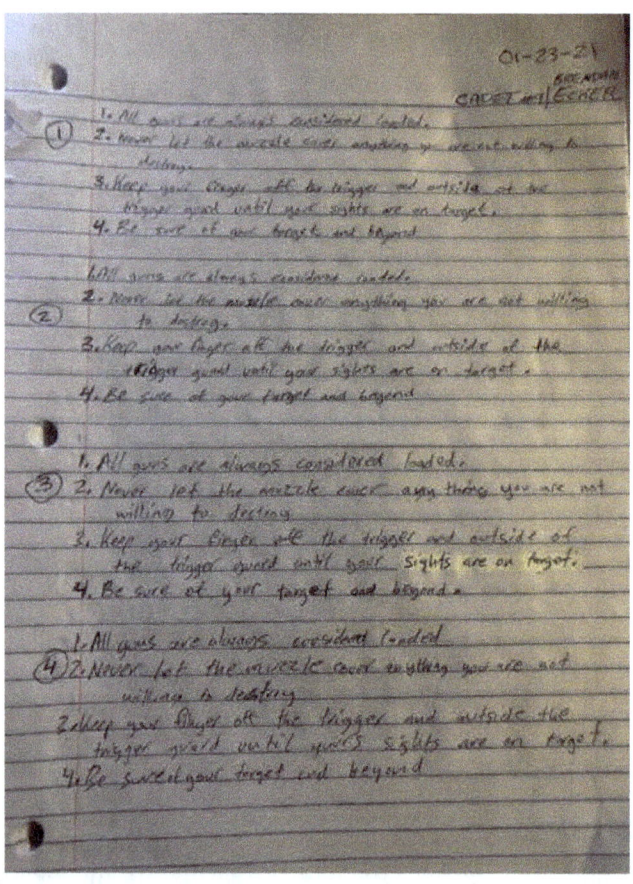

(5)
1. All guns are always considered loaded.
2. Never let the muzzle cover anything you are not willing to destroy.
3. Keep your finger off the trigger and outside of the trigger guard until your sights are on target.
4. Be sure of your target and beyond.

(6)
1. All guns are always considered loaded.
2. Never let the muzzle cover anything you are not willing to destroy.
3. Keep your finger off the trigger and outside of the trigger guard until your sights are on target.
4. Be sure of your target and beyond.

(7)
1. All guns are always considered loaded.
2. Never let the muzzle cover anything you are not willing to destroy.
3. Keep your finger off the trigger and outside of the trigger guard until your sights are on target.
4. Be sure of your target and beyond.

(8)
1. All guns are always considered loaded.
2. Never let the muzzle cover anything you are not willing to destroy.
3. Keep your finger off the trigger and outside of the trigger guard until your sights are on target.
4. Be sure of your target and beyond.

(9)
1. All guns are always considered loaded.
2. Never let the muzzle cover anything you are not willing to destroy.
3. Keep your finger off the trigger and outside of the trigger guard until your sights are on target.
4. Be sure of your target and beyond.

(10)
1. All guns are always considered loaded.
2. Never let the muzzle cover anything you are not willing to destroy.
3. Keep your finger off the trigger and outside of the trigger guard until your sights are on target.
4. Be sure of your target and beyond.

(11)
1. All guns are always considered loaded.
2. Never let the muzzle cover anything you are not willing to destroy.
3. Keep your finger off the trigger and outside of the trigger guard until your sights are on target.
4. Be sure of your target and beyond.

12)
1. All guns are always considered loaded.
2. Never let the muzzle cover anything you are not willing to destroy.
3. Keep your finger off the trigger and outside the trigger guard until your sights are on target.
4. Be sure of your target and beyond.

13)
1. All guns are always considered loaded.
2. Never let the muzzle cover anything you are not willing to destroy.
3. Keep your finger off the trigger and outside the trigger guard until your sights are on target.
4. Be sure of your target and beyond.

14)
1. All guns are always considered loaded.
2. Never let the muzzle cover anything you are not willing to destroy.
3. Keep your finger off the trigger and outside of the trigger guard until your sights are on target.
4. Be sure of your target and beyond.

15)
1. All guns are always considered loaded.
2. Never let the muzzle cover anything you are not willing to destroy.
3. Keep your finger off the trigger and outside of the trigger guard until your sights are on target.
4. Be sure of your target and beyond.

16)
1. All guns are always considered loaded.
2. Never let the muzzle cover anything you are not willing to destroy.
3. Keep your finger off the trigger and outside of the trigger and outside of the trigger guard until your sights are on target.
4. Be sure of your target and beyond.

17)
1. All guns are always considered loaded.
2. Never let the muzzle cover anything you are not willing to destroy.
3. Keep your finger off the trigger and outside of the trigger guard until your sights are on target.
4. Be sure of your target and beyond.

18)
1. All guns are always considered loaded.
2. Never let the muzzle cover anything you are not willing to destroy.
3. Keep your finger off the trigger and outside of the trigger guard until your sights are on target.
4. Be sure of your target and beyond.

19)
1. All guns are always considered loaded.
2. Never let the muzzle cover anything you are not willing to destroy.
3. Keep your finger off the trigger and outside of the trigger guard until your sights are on target.
4. Be sure of your target and beyond.

(20)
1. All guns are always considered loaded.
2. Never let the muzzle cover anything you are not willing to destroy.
3. Keep your finger off the trigger and outside of the trigger guard until your sights are on target.
4. Be sure of your target and beyond.

(21)
1. All guns are always considered loaded.
2. Never let the muzzle cover anything you are not willing to destroy.
3. Keep your finger off the trigger and outside of the trigger guard until your sights are on target.
4. Be sure of your target and beyond.

(22)
1. All guns are always considered loaded.
2. Never let the muzzle cover anything you are not willing to destroy.
3. Keep your finger off the trigger and outside of the trigger guard until your sights are on target.
4. Be sure of your target and beyond.

(23)
1. All guns are always considered loaded.
2. Never let the muzzle cover anything you are not willing to destroy.
3. Keep your finger off the trigger and outside of the trigger guard until your sights are on target.
4. Be sure of your target and beyond.

(24)
1. All guns are always considered loaded.
2. Never let the muzzle cover anything you are not willing to destroy.
3. Keep your finger off the trigger and outside of the trigger guard until your sights are on target.
4. Be sure of your target and beyond.

(25)
1. All guns are always considered loaded.
2. Never let the muzzle cover anything you are not willing to destroy.
3. Keep your finger off the trigger and outside of the trigger guard until your sights are on target.
4. Be sure of your target and beyond.

When we completed the assignment, we were then ready to get in the range and finally sling some lead. When we finally got into the firing range, we then went through a safety course and introduction to the firearms program and what to expect. We were instructed on how the daily inspections would be organized before loading up and starting the day. We were trained on basic terminology and common malfunctions with the firearms before ever firing a single round. We learned the three kinds of reloads (Administrative, Emergency, and Tactical). We learned to lock and load the weapon, and we learned the importance of sight alignment and sight pictures. We learned about tactical breathing and proper grip. Of course, we also learned about the several kinds of malfunctions possible with each weapon (Out of battery, stovepipes, double feeds) and how to fix any of the malfunctions by using the tap and rack method or the rip and pull method. We learned to "run the gun," "press check," and "unload and show clear" before ever being entrusted with firing live ammunition. We even learned how to reload our handguns using our belts or boot heels in case our firing hand or arm got shot. Everything in the police academy is carefully calculated segments of detailed training and focused preparation in order to mend muscle memory. As Abraham Lincoln once said, "if you give me 6 hours to cut down a tree, I will spend the first four sharpening the ax".

Typically, we would divide the class into two groups. One group would go to the gymnasium, where you would practice firearms handling and cleaning while being introduced to the following day's training. The other group would head to the range and qualify.

We started with the Glock 17. The required qualifications consisted of scoring adequately when firing from the hip (3 yards from target), in the close quarter's contact (3 yards front target), mid-range (7 yards from target), mid-range with barricade (7 yards from target), and long-range (12-15 yards from the target). Every academy is different, but this was our standard qualification.

Everyone qualified in both of my academies. We even had a top-shot competition where we would compete to see who could score the highest. I got 5th place in my first academy.

Firearms were one of the more fun parts of the academy experience and also extremely important. When firearms were done, and after everyone was successfully qualified, going on to about week 7, our class then began Emergency Vehicle Operations (E.V.O).

Emergency Vehicle Operations (Lights, Sirens, & Speed)

Emergency Vehicle Operations was probably my favorite part of the police academy. There's nothing quite like driving fast and whipping a Crown Victoria or 2021 Chevy Tahoe and doing it with emergency lights and sirens. I fucking loved E.V.O., and you will, too, when you get there. In Emergency Vehicle Operations, you learn how to safely drive hot to a call and control a police vehicle. You learn how to operate the patrol vehicle and activate its many features in order to do your job. These features you will become familiar with in E.V.O will be the vehicle's sirens, emergency lights, spot lights, take down lights, horn, Mobile Data Computer, P. A speaker, in-car cameras, and in-car radios.

In E.V.O, you'll start off with classroom lectures and a compilation of a million different videos on what to do and what not to do when driving hot to a call or just conducting a regular patrol in general. You learn how to call out a traffic stop, develop a traffic stop dialogue, search intentionally for the driver or passenger's hands, safely extract a driver or passenger from the vehicle, and how to tactically position and utilize your patrol vehicle when conducting a stop or response to a high-priority call. You'll learn how to communicate through the vehicle's radio. You learn it all, and it's a lot, but the best part is driving fast and spending a few days outside of the ordinary paramilitary atmosphere. You begin to get closer to the instructors and develop bonds with your classmates. You begin to earn a shred of respect from your instructors, and again - YOU GET TO GO FAST, as Ricky Bobby once said.

When you've passed your written E.V.O exam on how to safely do everything I just listed, then you'll get to actually go fast and apply what you've learned hands-on. My academy went to Selfridge Air Base to do our E.V.O. training. It was simple. On the first day, you meet your new instructors and split up into groups. You share a vehicle with 2 or 3 people, and you'll practice the course. The course consists of the serpentine, evasive maneuver, reverse driving, 90-degree turn, brake-and-steer, and then brief training on how to conduct a traffic stop. You and your group will then take turns driving while the others in the group will pick up cones that are knocked over. Overall, it is a laid-back three days of just driving fast, enjoying the fresh air, and bonding with the instructors. I remember having a blast in both academies I graduated from.

After E.V.O., you are introduced to subject control. Remember, during all of these training courses I've told you about, every single morning, you have been attending P.T every day still, running a minimum of a mile per day, while preparing for the MCOLES final PT exam - so don't think that you won't still be sore and exhausted. At the end of E.V.O., your entire class runs a course incorporating every evolution. Before moving on to the next phase of the academy, after three days of going fast and whipping a police cruiser, you compete for who can drive the fastest serpentine. Interestingly enough, the individual who failed the state licensing exam with me the first time around in my first academy was the winner of this competition. It is still a bummer that he never persisted in becoming a police officer, as he was one of our academy's finest cadets.

First Aid, Fight Club, & Graduation

At this point in the academy, you are introduced to First Aid and Subject Control, or as we called it, Fight Club. Both of these courses were generally close together in terms of time. From what I remember, First Aid was easy but boring - and you had to score at least an 80% on this exam. When you completed First Aid, then you would move on to Subject Control. In my academy, we learned Krav Maga as our primary fighting style. As stated earlier, many academies will vary in what kind of fighting style they will choose, some choosing Krav Maga, some Brazilian Jiu Jitsu, and some learning system in rare cases.

For subject control, we would go to the gymnasium every day and start off by running around the facility for about 10-20 minutes in our gear belts to get comfortable hauling the weight of it on our bodies. We were getting comfortable with being uncomfortable for the most part. You would partner up with someone of your choice and spar with them to practice the different moves taught in the class. In my first academy, my partner was a guy named Ray. He was an afro-haired musician who had a way with the guitar before he cleaned up and found himself in the police academy. In my second academy, my partner was the girl I had briefly dated in the academy. I figured if I was going to be rolling around with someone on the mat for the remainder of the academy, I definitely would rather do it with a girl I was dating at the time. Subject control was fun overall, but it was, of course, exhausting and a lot of work.

For the final exam, we took a written exam that we were required to score at least a 70% on, then we were to complete a hands-on exam (not hard to pass if you tried). Subject Control was one of the more fun areas in the academy, and it was vital to survival as a police officer. Obviously, you must know how to defend yourself if you plan on making it as a cop. You don't have to be Bruce Lee, but you should be able to defend yourself with basic and simple styles of self-defense.

If I had the choice, I would have rather learned Brazilian Jiu-Jitsu over Krav Maga due to the versatile and superior methods of subject containment. In Jiu-Jitsu, you are trained in various methods to control any subject by simple and proven submissions and reversals. In Krav Maga, you are trained in more striking-focused fighting. In today's era, with the mainstream media targeting Law Enforcement for any and all appearances of excessive force - striking is a terrible look when millions see it on T.V. Jiu Jitsu is more of a sparring and wrestling defense method, and it appears as if the officer is doing everything in their power to avoid punching or kicking the subject when in reality, this is far more effective and painful to the subject when fallen victim to the mixed martial art. In its entirety, both methods are effective, but one is simply better for Law Enforcement in terms of avoiding lawsuits and causing a media frenzy.

When you have finally passed your written and physical examination for Subject Control, then you will find yourself moving on to the next phase of the academy - tactical operations, terrorism, and homeland security, OC spray certification, and sometimes taser certification. In the middle of this phase, you will do many scenario days, as you will at the beginning of your chosen police academy.

In tactical operations, at least at the academy I attended, we worked excessively on how to respond to active shooter events, terrorist events, close-quarters response, and deadly force situations. Throughout the entire academy, we conducted simulated training through MILO and hands-on mock evolutions.

Lastly, after all of this hard work, eventually, you would take your final exam to test your knowledge of everything you learned in the Academy. It is required that you have a 70% or higher on the final exam for the police academy to graduate. At least the one I attended was like this. If you did not pass, you would have one more chance to pass that test. If you failed twice, you would have to start all the way back at the beginning. I passed the final exam and was able to graduate from both police academies I attended. Where I stumbled was the state licensing exam, which follows the final exam, and happens one day before your academy graduation ceremony.

Chapter 10: The State Licensing Exam: Adversity

The state licensing exam was much harder than the final exam. Some people may disagree, but in my opinion, the state exam was much harder because you didn't know how you did on the test, and simply because the fact that your entire Law Enforcement future depended on the exam itself made it that much harder and stressful (at least in my opinion). Each answer was very similar. Although you would only have three options of multiple choice questions on the test itself, two of the questions were very similar answers, and one of them was obviously wrong. I remember the day of my interview to get accepted into the police academy, hearing some of the current cadets that were in the class talking about the state exam. Right from the get-go, I was not looking forward to taking that test.

After graduating from my first police academy, I failed the state licensing exam when I took it the following day after graduation. Strike one. A week later, when I retook the exam, I failed it again by one point. That was my second and final strike. I remember both times getting a call from my Director. The first time he had said, "Brendan, unfortunately, you did not pass the state exam. I'm very sorry." A week later, I got another phone call after retaking the exam. I really believed I had passed. I believe I had studied hard enough.

However, it was the same thing. "Brendan, I'm very sorry, but you did not pass the state licensing exam. I feel horrible."

The second time hearing this was the hardest. It was the hardest because my mom was in the room at the time and was so excited to see me succeed. It was one of the darkest moments in my entire life. I was at a loss for words and couldn't believe I had really failed a second time. I even remember feeling like I was in a dream at the moment. It didn't feel real. I remember saying out loud after I hung up the phone, "Well. I'm never going to be a police officer". I felt like I wasted all of that time and had nothing to show for it. No money, no girl, no success - just defeat.

When I was still on the phone with my Director, I remember asking, "What do I do now?". The Director told me that I would have to restart the Academy from the very beginning but would still be able to do it again free of charge. For the second option, I was told that he could put me in contact with a corrections Sergeant for the county sheriff's office so I could still get a job as a correctional officer. I remember telling the Director that I would have to think about it. I remember asking if anybody else had failed, and if I was the only one. Fortunately, I wasn't the only failure at the time. The same cadet in that first academy that won the serpentine competition for our E.V.O class was the same cadet who had failed the state exam with me.

Originally, there were two other cadets in my class that had failed the state licensing exam with me the first time around. One of those cadets did end up passing the licensing exam after retaking the exam, and two of us failed it a second time. However, only one of us chose to do the Academy all over again.

The other cadet chose not to return to the Academy. He was a bodybuilder and one of our best cadets in the class. To this day, I still feel bad because he texted me, and I never texted him back. I still couldn't believe that I had failed. I hadn't failed in anything in my entire life. The bodybuilder was ranked in the middle of the class in terms of GPA. I remember that I was third to last. At the end of the day, despite this, only one of us chose to give up, and one of us chose to keep going.

The night that I had failed the exam was probably one of the worst of my entire life, undoubtedly. I did not sleep. I remember the group chat from my police academy at the time, all celebrating their success. Only me and the other person who failed were silent in the group chat. It didn't take long for everybody to know. I already knew that they had probably started a separate group chat just to talk about how I and the other cadet had failed the exam twice. It was also one of the most embarrassing things I'd ever gone through in my life. I shut off my phone and shut myself out from the world.

Fortunately, it was good weather at the time, so I bought a 12-pack of Bud Light (before it was woke), some charcoal fluid, and a fire starter, and said, "Fuck it." I sat by my bonfire with my mom and just drank the sorrow away. The entire night I kept asking myself, "What do I do now?" I had just finished the credits for my bachelor's degree in criminal justice, so on the bright side, I always had options in terms of which career I wanted to pursue if not a police officer.

At the very least, I still had my degree because I had successfully graduated from the Academy. In my eyes, it could've been worse, as I could've failed the final exam for the Academy twice too many times, which would have resulted in me never getting my bachelor's degree at all. If that were to happen, not only would I have to go back to college and graduate later than everybody else I knew, but there would also be the lingering idea that I wouldn't be able to attend the Academy again at all.

As I kept drinking my beer and wondering about what my future looked like, I finally made up my mind. I was going to do the Academy again. I was going to suffer through it, and I was going to succeed.

The day after I failed the state licensing exam, I asked the Director if he would allow me to conduct a tour with the corrections sergeant at the sheriff's office jail anyways, just in case I had changed my mind about doing the academy again. I was honored that my Director had even considered putting me in contact with someone else so I could actually get something out of my failure. I remember dressing up in my suit and going through the motions. I met the sergeant, got a tour of the jail, and met a few other officers. However, this never changed my mind. I was going to do that police academy a second time, and I was going to succeed. I was born to be a cop, at least for a short time, so I accepted my failure and chose to transform it into success.

It was at this time that I contacted my Director and notified him that I wanted to do the Academy again. I remember saying, "Let's do this." From there, nothing else mattered but success to me. The next day, everyone who passed the state exam was excited and celebrating their success. I remember the entire day, simply feeling horrible. I walked into the classroom, and eventually, people began to ask questions. I told him the truth. And what did they say? "Dude, I'm sorry. I would kill myself if I didn't pass that exam". "Haha, Brendan, you're such an idiot. I can't believe you failed." "Hey, at least you're doing it again. Glad I'm not you. I would never do this academy again".

I couldn't believe the lack of support I had from the people I had suffered with throughout this entire experience, especially when we all struggled in different areas of that Academy together. I was expecting them to lift me up, but instead, all I remember was getting shot down and kicked when I was already feeling low. I learned a lot from that day. I learned that you can't rely on others to support your vision or goals, especially when you take a temporary loss. It's your life. I wasn't a pussy about their perception of me. The lack of support never bothered me. It has always been on me to prove the doubters and haters wrong. When it comes to any great achievement in life, when the stakes are high, and the odds are stacked against you, all you have is yourself and your willingness to endure the pain - and then win with no mercy or second thoughts.

None of them cared about my failure; in fact, they almost enjoyed it to a small extent. That is how the world is. The world is filled with cynicism and negativity. Filled with spectators who believe they know who you are and see you the way they wish to see you. You cannot control this. You can only change it by determination, strength, focus, and relentless execution of your goals - no matter what it takes. All of my false friends and supporters in my first academy acted as if they never even knew me and showed almost no support. I was astonished by this, but I never let it get to me.

The truth is, life doesn't give a fuck about your failures. Life doesn't give a fuck about when things get hard. The world is out to destroy you if you let it, and you have to be okay with taking your licks and taking the hits. You have to be ruthlessly aggressive and selfish for your own success, just as everyone else is. Nobody else is going to accomplish your goals for you. When you fail and when you fall, you can either quit or you can get back up and keep going until you rise again. That is the game of life and the secret to winning at it. The game of winning in life is cyclical in nature and measured by long-term gains, not short-term losses. There is no such thing as failure, only success.

So on the day of my graduation ceremony, I didn't take anything to heart. I smiled and showed the respect that was due to my peers who had succeeded. After all, they succeeded because they studied harder and played the game better than I did. I accepted this and decided that I was going to do the same thing and work even harder to achieve that goal I had set out to accomplish.

I refused to allow anything to distract me from my overall goal. I celebrated their success with genuine pride and enthusiasm because that was the honorable thing to do and the right thing to do. I knew from that moment that I was about to do great things and that I would never let short-term losses get in my way. I was going to stay focused, I was going to do better than I did the first time, and I was going to win. I was going to earn the badge no matter what it took. I truly cared about helping people, and I wanted to be a cop the day that I gave up on my dreams of being a Navy Seal in High School. I was not going to fail again, and it was that simple.

Fast forward to an entirely new police academy; just a few months after failing the state licensing exam in my first academy, I was with a brand new bunch of cadets. This time, I was ready. I knew exactly what to expect, and I knew exactly what to do. I decided that not only was I going to crush the state licensing exam, but I was going to be a leader and make sure nobody else failed that exam. I was going to make sure that nobody else had the same feeling that I felt. And wouldn't you know it, everyone in my second police academy passed their state licensing exam. We all won together, and today, they are all accomplished individuals and exceptional police officers. It was time to finally move on to the next step that I had been waiting so long for - getting hired.

Public Service Institute
MACOMB COMMUNITY COLLEGE

Discover. Connect. *Advance.*

Criminal Justice Training Center
presents this
CERTIFICATE of TRAINING
to

Brendan Ecker

who has successfully completed 778 hours of instruction in

Basic Police Academy

given this 13th day of December 2021

Chapter 11: Getting Hired

Getting hired is the next step after you've accomplished the grueling challenge of succeeding through both the Academy and the several examinations that come with it. Now, it's showtime. This is when it all matters the most and where all the hard work pays off. I remember failing my state licensing exam twice too many times after my first academy, and I still did what I could to get hired as a cop. I did everything I could to work my way around the hurdle without having to put in the work all over again, but it was a lost cause, and I was sent out the door and told, "Go back to the academy and pass the state exam, and come back when you've done it." Ironically, this was the Sheriff's department where I was later hired at. Before I could earn the badge, I had to meet the prerequisites and get my MCOLES number, and so I did.

When I did finally graduate from my second academy, I sent another email to the Lieutenant of the same Sheriff's Office I had applied to 6 months prior. This time I got the job, but it took almost three months for me to finally get the news that I was hired. It was a long process, and I felt like it almost wasn't even worth going through two academies at times. I sent my email, and the next thing I knew, I was contacted by my hiring Sergeant, who I still call a friend today. He had contacted me with a phone call and asked if I would be able to do a home visit.

A home visit is where your hiring officer comes to your house to interview you and, of course, observes how your living situation is. They check out whether your house is clean or messy while simultaneously reviewing whether or not you are a good fit for their department. They ask you about your work history, why you want to become a police officer, and why you deserve the job over someone else who is currently applying for the job. In my first interview, before I had actually passed the state licensing exam, I never had an answer to the question, "Why do you deserve this job over our other applicants." In my second interview, which was during the home visit, I did have an answer.

Obviously, my answer was that I was the only person I knew who graduated from the police academy twice in a row, despite the hard work it took and the sacrifices I made. I proved that I wanted it through my sagacious drive and relentless desire to Succeed. I explained how in the locker room during the academy when my classmates and I were discussing it, about 70% of my class said they would never do the academy again if they had failed the state exam, even if the academy were free of cost. They said that even if they were paid $100,000 to do the academy all over again, they still wouldn't do it. This was how it was in both academies that I attended. They didn't want it as badly as I did. It meant more to me than it did to them, and that was my exact answer.

I remember my home visit went fairly well. My house was a mess before my interview, and I was rushing as fast as possible to get it cleaned. Fortunately, my house looked spotless when the day of the home visit arrived. When my interview was over, the next step was making it through the scenario days.

Usually, most police departments don't require that new hires complete a series of scenario days, but mine did. I won't lie. I hated the scenario days. To me, they were very counterintuitive and very unhelpful for me personally. It always seemed like it was merely an opportunity for other officers to humiliate you, laugh at your mistakes, and continue to embarrass the cadet, while strangers would act foolish just because they had a chance to be an actor for an hour or two. But that's just my opinion on scenario days. I could not stand them, and I remember always lying when asked if they were helpful (because, as a cop, you have to lie to your superiors when they ask if their scenarios are helpful). For other officers, scenario days were very helpful, so they claimed, and if so, that is all that matters. For me, I hated them!

Fortunately, I made it through them and checked it off the list. Next was the worst part, in my opinion, which was the psychological evaluations, which we discussed earlier in this book. After the psychological evaluations came to the drug test, and finally, you were hired and asked to come pick up your gear and get sized for your uniforms, which was the best part and an amazing feeling. When you had finally been hired, after all the additional hard work beyond the academy, then it was time to start FTO. This was one of my biggest struggles, and unfortunately, I never made it through my first FTO process.

Chapter 12: Keeping the Job: FTO (Field Training Officer)

As much as I would love to lie and say that I succeeded in my first-ever FTO process, I cannot say that. I washed out after 2.5 months of working for my dream department. It sucked, but it built a big part of my character and awakened me to just how difficult the job of being a police officer truly is. I had finally made it, and I even remember my hiring Sergeant saying to me in his office, "Brendan — you fucking did it!" For me to fail and not cut, it was hard for me to take, as I had always been motivated and prevailed through any challenge that arose. This time was different, and I'm going to tell you all about it so you can prepare yourself and avoid the same mistakes that I made.

This chapter is about keeping the job as a police officer. Although I did not keep my first job, and although I eventually quit my second job as a police officer to become an entrepreneur and author, I still know what it takes to keep the job and bypass some of the setbacks I went through in my Law Enforcement experience. This book is about discussing my successes and failures in my journey of being a police officer. I wrote this book to educate aspiring police officers and entrepreneurs like myself. I want to talk about the details of what I stumbled on during my journey so that you will hopefully never make the same mistakes that I did. Let us begin.

There were 3 phases to FTO, which is better known as Field Training Officer, each of those phases taking about one month. On your first day, you go to your department and get all of your necessary gear. You will get a binder filled with evaluation reports and a binder for your FTO's evaluation reports. You will then get your firearm, taser, OC spray, holsters, handcuffs, flashlight, keepers, radio, duty belt, bulletproof vest, latex gloves, uniform shirt, uniform pants, uniform hat, and of course, your badges, and keys to the department building and local schools.

In phase one, you are expected to handle about 10%-20% of the workload as you shadow another officer or deputy for the few weeks starting out. You are learning your way around the county or city, learning how your FTO handles different kinds of calls, and basically getting a feel for the department you are working at. You're learning how to use the MDC (Mobile Data Computer) in your patrol vehicle, getting a refresher course on the laws of your state, and getting the go-around of how reports are to be written at your department. You really aren't expected to know a whole lot. You're the "rookie," the "new guy," "boot," or "cub," depending on the language of your department and the type of police officer you are.

In phase two, the pressure gets heavier, and the workload gets larger. You're now responsible for handling about 20%-50% of the workload. By the end of phase two, you're basically handling the calls yourself, with some minor assistance from your FTO. It is usually in phase two or late phase one when you'll do your first D.U.I investigation, which is one of the more time-consuming and detail-oriented investigations police officers handle. At this point, you are expected to know when and when not to activate your emergency lights and sirens. You're expected to know how to approach domestic violence calls and how to handle them, as well as what procedures are to take place. You're expected to know a general basis of knowledge for any call that you go to. You are expected to know how to write and properly distribute tickets, search warrants, arrest warrants, tabulations, mental petitions, voluntary or refusal DI-177 forms, witness statements, driver reevaluation forms, missing person forms, sexual assault forms, impound slips, CFS reports, and basic field reports.

In phase three, you are now handling anywhere from 50% to 100% of the calls. Essentially, your FTO will sit in the passenger seat, and they will say nothing. You'll be expected to answer any calls that come over the radio, handle the calls completely yourself, and make minimal mistakes doing it. At this point, you are expected to know the job at full capacity without assistance from another officer.

I, for one, never felt as if I had even had a chance to learn the job. I had washed out of the FTO program at my first sheriff's department after just 2.5 months. I simply just wasn't ready, and I was expected to be ready, even when I hadn't even handled ten priority calls yet. I couldn't believe that I was expected to practically know the entire job of being a cop, expected to handle every call myself, after only wearing the badge for less than three months. I was just a rookie cop with zero law enforcement experience aside from a few ride-along with Detroit City P.D. in high school and two internships with this same Sheriff's Department.

Even when I was in phase two, I still never felt like I was ever getting guidance from anyone. I remember asking a question and then receiving more questions in the form of "answers." I was treated like an idiot by everyone when all I was trying to do was learn the job. As you can guess, my questions hardly ever got answered. I remember asking what to do in certain situations and only receiving a "you should already know that" or "what do you think the answer is" response. I could not believe how poor the leadership was at this first department, and every day was worse than the last.

One of the deputies that I had ridden along with took 15 minutes just to give me the answer to a question he had asked that I obviously didn't know. He allowed me to sit in the driver's seat for 15 minutes, not knowing the answer to his question, only so he could insult me further and laugh at my rookie ignorance. I learned absolutely nothing from him and wasted my time completely. He was a horrible influence, and I remember thinking to myself, "God, I never want to be like him."

This was the same as another FTO I had, who answered every single question I had with more questions that I didn't know the answers to. It was extremely frustrating and weird, considering that I had never had a problem getting my questions answered and learning before getting hired as a police officer. Almost every cop was like this, besides two other Field Training Officers that I had worked with, who were absolutely outstanding FTOs. I can only remember two FTOs who truly wanted me to get better and actually taught me a great deal about how to be a great cop. Everyone else, however, only seemed to enjoy watching me struggle and fail. It was very different from any other job or sport that I learned to master with the help of mentors, coaches, teammates, or employers. This was one of the only instances where it seemed like I was all on my own and expected to learn everything by myself, with zero help whatsoever.

It was almost like nobody ever wanted to help me, and I remember just feeling depressed and angry every night I would come home. I would feel like a failure, and I would feel like I was letting everyone down who believed in me. I would study hard and just pray that it would get a little bit better each day. And it was the same thing every day until my last day working at that first sheriff's department. I had learned fast that I was not where I belonged and that I deserved better.

This was at my first department, which was the sheriff's department I dreamed of working at for years at this point. I remember being marked down for everything. I remember even being marked down because I left the windshield wipers on when it wasn't raining. It got so bad that I was literally paranoid to even roll down my window, worrying that I would possibly be marked down for that. One of the biggest things I remember was that I was constantly annoyed by that same FTO in the passenger seat, hearing the click of the pen, and scribbles of the paper, almost every five minutes, it seemed. I hated hearing that click of the pen in what felt like every 5 minutes. I couldn't even focus because all I remember was thinking, "shit, what did I do wrong this time" or "fuck, there's another thing I messed up." It was one of the worst experiences I had to endure, especially given the fact that I had worked so hard just to get to this point.

Granted, as stated before, I have my own faults as well. I made a lot of mistakes being a dumb rookie with not a clue of how to do the job. I ran a red light at one point because I was so stressed and flustered from a prior call that I had gone to. On another occasion, I had even backed into a patrol vehicle in my last two weeks at that first sheriff's department. To make matters worse, my cousin (who is also a Police Officer) was there to see the whole thing with at least a half dozen other officers. This had taken place at central dispatch, so even the dispatchers walked out to see it. I remember it being pitch black and hearing the clash of my patrol vehicle and the one parked directly behind mine. As I got out of the vehicle, my FTO (one of the better FTOs I mentioned earlier) got out of the car and radioed to the other officers in dispatch. The next thing I knew, everyone was outside and laughing at my mistake. At this point, I knew I was totally and completely fucked. I was embarrassed and knew that my time in this department was going to be short-lived, if not over already. But, I kept my cool and remained as professional as I could at that moment.

As you can see, I was not perfect by any means, and I struggled a lot when I first started out as a rookie cop, but when I think about it all again, I still believe that it wasn't all my fault. Being a man who has always held himself accountable for his own mistakes and never blamed other people, this was the first time in my life that I did, and I still do. I still believe there was a better way to teach and a better way to lead a new recruit. Out of all of the sports teams I played for in my life, the powerlifting meets I had won, and all of the classes I attended as an honor student in college, truthfully, I had never seen such a poor leadership structure as bad as the first department that I had worked for. I felt more bullied than I was welcomed by the guys and girls I was supposed to trust with my life. I wish I could say differently. Was I a dumb rookie in some regard? Yes. Absolutely. No doubt about it. I take the blame for a lot of it. But in my limited experience, it was more of a leadership problem than it was a problem learning or comprehending the job, mainly, as stated, because I was never given a chance to learn.

Even though I graduated from two consecutive academies, the police academy only teaches you so much. They didn't teach us how to use mobile data computers, LEIN, or your radio systems. The academy that I attended taught you the very basics. On the scenario days, we would run a lot of basic scenarios that never truly challenged you like many of the calls you'd go to on the real job. Oftentimes, during many of the scenario days that I went through, both in my academy and at my first sheriff's department, the role players would fall out of character and eventually start acting moronic and stupid, totally unrelated to the fact pattern in the scenario, completely defeating the purpose of creating a real-life simulation. When you made a mistake during the scenario, the officers in charge of the scenarios would either laugh at you or make you feel like an idiot completely — again, defeating the purpose of the scenario itself and overmatching the ability to learn.

The purpose of any scenario is to learn from your mistakes and to teach the recruits how to better handle such life-endangering situations. The best training scenarios I ever did as a cadet and cop were the MILO (Multiple Interactive Learning Objectives) based training because the situations were far more realistic to what you would see as an active duty cop, with role players who remained accurate to the character in the fact pattern of the given scenario. But I digress.

Unfortunately, as stated before, I eventually resigned from that first sheriff's department that I had dreamed of working at for years. I remember the feeling of finishing all my reports that I had left, clearing any CFS'(Calls for Service) I still had pending and waiting in the conference room for nearly 2 hours just to get the news that I wouldn't be moving on to phase three. I was given the option to resign, and of course, I took it gratefully.

I remember being crushed to my core but also very relieved at the same time. I never dared to shed a tear because it wasn't worth it. I had worked my ass off and graduated from two consecutive academies, made it through the grueling hiring process of becoming a police officer, only so

I could be told, "We're sorry, you're just not cutting it." It sucked, but even with the unfortunate situation, I was still so grateful just to have the opportunity of learning the job and actually working at the department I had dreamed of working in for years. I left with class. I thanked my superiors, smiled, told them I had no hard feelings and began to pack my things for the end of my journey at the sheriff's department.

In many ways, I was actually glad to be done with it. I was ready to try for a different department more suitable to what I was looking for as a cop. Even my superiors had told me that I just needed more experience and that I started off in an advanced department with advanced officers with a lifetime of experience behind them. Before I even left the property, I was already referred to a smaller department in the same county by one of my fellow deputies at the time. I left on great terms, and I still respect everyone in that department because many of them were outstanding police officers, just not the best leaders. I packed up my gear, gathered my uniforms, gave them to my hiring sergeant, shook his hand one last time, and made my way out to start fresh somewhere new.

During my time at that sheriff's department, I arrested two drunks, handled a handful of domestic violence calls, responded 105 mph to around four different PIAs (Personal Injury Accidents), a few Larcenies, and of course, to the officer-involved shooting where I was originally supposed to be on that call with my FTO (he had a dentist appointment when this occurred). The officer-involved shooting was on my fourth day being hired as a sheriff's deputy. Thank God that the deputy is still alive and well, and made a full recovery after being shot three times. He was eventually awarded the Medal of Valor a little over a year later. That same deputy was the husband of one of my elementary school teachers.

The next department that I later worked for, which was the last department that I worked for as a full-time police officer, didn't even have an FTO program. The pay was better than the sheriff's department that I had worked for. I had decent insurance and a 401k that they would put 8% of your check into (which I never used because I was always an investor, so I collected as much cash as I could for real estate and my businesses). It was more of a "Here's your gun, here's your badge, stay safe, now go out and have some fun" kind of department. The department had just two officers working there at the time, including the Chief. It was a small-town police department in Sanilac County, Michigan. After riding along with the Chief for about two weeks, I was left alone to do my own thing, and I absolutely loved it. I learned more from this "training program" than from the nationally standard FTO program.

There wasn't much to it. The stress in my life was completely gone at this point. I was already used to working 12-hour shifts, handling mind-numbing complaints, and driving hot to a call in what felt like every 15 minutes, so for me to move to a small town department with 8-hour shifts was fairly simple, and it was pretty enjoyable. It was nice to go to work, not have to talk to any coworkers, not half to deal with being marked down for windshield wipers, and just get to know people in your community. It was nice when I was able to just sit in my patrol vehicle, patrol around, keep things in check, and listen to my business podcasts over Bluetooth.

The reason I later left this department was essentially because I was just tired of being a cop. I wanted to make money, a lot of it, and I wanted to have the time and freedom to work on my businesses and projects. This book, for example, was written as I was a police officer at the same department. It took me forever to finish it, mainly because I was working five days a week and exhausted from the graveyard night shift. Not to mention, I was starting to lose passion for the job itself. Although I hadn't been a cop for long, I still just wasn't in the game the way I always wanted to be. My boss was pretty great, and the pay was very livable, but eventually, politics had gotten in the way, and I was put on part-time for incorrectly calling out a BOL (Be On Lookout), among other internal reasons that I won't get into.

The point is I had a blast in that department, and I learned a lot working there. I will always be grateful for how beneficial and character-building the experience was, but I soon decided that I was more committed to the Freedom and Independence of being an entrepreneur. I wanted to be rich more than I wanted to work a 9-5 and stay capped on wealth creation for my entire life. I wanted time to enjoy my life, and I wanted control over my life. To me, I enjoyed the feeling of helping more people, in a more indirect way, through content creation and publishing my books, for example. I loved the grind of modern-day wealth creation through the many unconventional ways to buy time over a "decent pension," which was through e-commerce, freelancing, day trading, buying businesses, real estate investing, and affiliate marketing. These were far more beneficial uses of my time and allowed me to achieve so much more in life than I knew I was capable of.

I was always more of an entrepreneur, truth be told. Before I ever became a police officer, and before I ever chose criminal justice as my major in college, I was a phenomenal writer and investor, loved starting businesses, and, more than anything, enjoyed the rush that came with being an entrepreneur. There are many other reasons that I became an entrepreneur, but many of those reasons will be covered in this book and already have been covered. This chapter is about my experience in FTO, what I learned from my time as a cop, and how to keep the job as a cop if you so choose.

In a nutshell, FTO is hard in any department. No matter how great of a cop you are, no matter how fast you think, you are always worrying about fucking up. That's the nature of this business. This is a professional career. Therefore, you need to be a consummate professional, and you need to be fast on your feet. This isn't to say that I wasn't, but my issue was that I simply had zero experience. I truly didn't know how to handle any of these calls yet, despite the many scenarios I had done in the Academy. It took me about 6 or 7 months before I became confident enough to do the job correctly and with satisfactory speed, swagger, confidence, and gusto.

It is important to understand that if you want to make it through FTO and if you want to keep your job as a cop, then you need to be enterprising and have a magnetic personality. The officers around you and the community members you take an oath to serve want to know that they can joke around with you and connect with you at a human level. They want to be able to trust you and develop a professional friendship with you.

You also need to be excellent at making decisions and making them quickly. You will find that during your time as a police officer, and especially during FTO, you will be graded on your ability to make difficult decisions quickly and to the best of your ability while simultaneously not breaking the law. In other words, learn to think fast on your feet and make sure you have a good understanding of the laws in your state.

The laws are always changing in every state, no matter which state you live in. This is why it is so critical for a police officer to constantly stay updated and informed on the ever-changing legislation and case law being implemented and enforced. You'll be graded on your ability to know the law, which is something I also struggled with as a recruit. Although I knew the law to a fair extent as a rookie cop, I did not get scores that met the "Level 7" ranking in my FTO evaluations, which was the highest-ranking performance you could get. I mostly got 3s, 4s, and 5s during most areas of my FTO evaluation period. You were required to reach the "Level 4 or higher" ranking in each training area for the evaluations by the end of your 3rd month's FTO period.

You have to be thick-skinned when you finally get hired and make your way to FTO and, eventually, on your own in the patrol vehicle. You have to be good at taking criticism and fearless to walk into a room and take control of a chaotic situation. Even when you're wrong and when you don't know what to do, you have to be willing to make a call and be a leader at the moment. People are relying on you to be a hero, a mediator, a guardian, and a peacemaker - so be that person. As a police officer, you are the chosen one by God to bring peace when there is a lack thereof. You are responsible for containing an emergency and maintaining order. You are dealing with people on their worst days. This is precisely why, in these dangerous situations, when we as police officers throw ourselves into Hellish moments that carry the risk of injury and death, being able to make decisions quickly and swiftly is so important. It is one of the most important parts of the FTO program because it will carry into your career as a cop both on duty and off duty. Get good at making decisions safely, quickly, correctly, and swiftly.

Multitasking is another facet of making decisions quickly, and it's another very important part of being a police officer. You have a lot going on when you're responding to Domestic Violence, Assault and Battery, Breaking and Entering, Armed Robbery, Active Shooting, Kidnapping, Hot Pursuit, or any emergency call for that matter. You'll be using the GPS on your MDC while communicating with dispatch through your radio while toggling through your emergency lights, horns, and sirens, while also scanning your surroundings for pedestrians, oncoming traffic, and additional threats or persons matching a description put out by dispatch - all the while, driving at dangerous speeds of 90-115 MPH. When you arrive on the scene, you've activated your body camera while continuously listening to and transcribing information through the radio, scanning your sectors, while remaining ready for hostile action at all times. Keep in mind while all of this is occurring, you will also be documenting addresses, vehicle license plates, dates of birth, and phone numbers, taking photographs and videos, and being sure to obtain witness statements and verbal testimonies. Not to mention, you're also communicating with your partners, securing the overall perimeter, and detaining subjects if necessary while distributing the correct and necessary documents to each party on scene.

The reason we police officers must become masters of these characteristics, skills, and qualities is for the sole purpose of defending our fellow man properly and adequately. When it comes to honoring the oath we take as police officers, these abilities are beyond imperative. The job of a police officer or sheriff's deputy is highly stressful and extremely nerve-racking. The job is ugly, tiring, and laborious. When you are wearing that uniform, you are the blue line that stands between the forces of good and evil in the human race. You are the wall that hatred and anarchy break against. You are the angel sent by God when the Devil comes out to play and scheme. You have an obligation to be ready at all times, and you have to be willing to love the suck, embrace the pain, and fight through the strain.

If you want to keep your job as a police officer, then you have to dedicate a lifetime to becoming a master at everything I have mentioned. If you are unwilling to give a large part of your life to this profession, dedicating yourself to the mission of maintaining order, defending the innocent, and getting little back in return, then this profession is unlikely for you. If that is the case, then you can always become something else that brings you pride and joy. As far as keeping your job goes, serving as a Law Enforcement professional, then this is the required way to do it.

When my career as a police officer was over, I chose the life of an entrepreneur, investor, author, and content creator, as I can still carry many of the same qualities and skills I mentioned into the world of book publication, commerce, real estate, and business. You have to be quick-brained, fearless, wise, discerning, enterprising, and industrious in any career you choose. You have to have a mindset of both a warrior and a guardian. You have to understand human psychology to an extraordinary extent and become an expert in de-escalation tactics if you choose the route of a Law Enforcement officer.

Lastly, to conclude this chapter, I cannot go on without emphasizing how important it is, whether you are a police officer, employee, or entrepreneur, to not be an idiot in life, simply put. This is the fastest way out of any job or career. Mistakes will happen, and there will always be a learning curve to any art or mastery. However, there is a difference between making mistakes at the beginning of any venture or career and learning from them versus downright being a fool and squandering the opportunity of living a life worth living.

For example, as a police officer, I've seen many friends and fellow officers ruin their lives and their careers. Many officers I have known have ruined their lives by allowing the job to consume them. They endure the hardships of the job and then resort to the bottle for answers. They fall into feelings of depression and let themselves go. I've seen some officers lose their jobs from being dumb enough to drink and drive, leading to the handcuffs clicking on their wrists with a mugshot backing it up. You see the videos on YouTube all the time. An officer is pulled over on a standard traffic stop, failing the series of Standard Field Sobriety Tests that they have administered on other civilians, and suddenly, that same officer finds themselves in the back of a cop car. The irony hits them when they have to call their loved ones and ask them to bail them out of jail. Do you really want to be that person? This is an example of being foolish, and it's a great way to lose your job as a cop. Not only that, but you will humiliate yourself and destroy your credibility, reputation, and public image. Do not be that person.

I can't stress it enough. If you are a police officer, you are held to a higher standard. You are expected to abide by the laws you swear an oath to defend and enforce. You are not above the law. You are still a civilian as a police officer.

You are not a military veteran who has earned the right to call themselves a soldier, and even in that case, soldiers must be just as careful not to shame the honor they have earned. One of the greatest mistakes I have seen fellow officers and veterans make is falling into the habit of drinking high contents of alcohol in order to numb the pain.

Drinking or using drugs is the fastest way to destroy not just any career but also your life. Although I myself was a social drinker early in my Law Enforcement career, I learned early on as a student-athlete in college that it was a horrible way to remain productive and healthy and a great way to waste time and subtract years off my life. I learned that I got more done when I replaced drinking with training and staying physically fit, which I will cover more in the next chapter.

If you want to keep your job as a police officer, or whatever it is you choose to become a master in, you must never allow yourself to become like those fools who waste their gifts. God can giveth, and he can taketh away. If you have a good job that you like, do your best to keep that job and be a master of it. If you have a great job, such as a police officer, then do everything you can to keep that job and not embarrass yourself or your family name. Bring homage and honor to your family name, as well as yourself and the children you will later birth. Honor yourself and respect yourself. Take the road less traveled and be a leader to those around you. If you choose to make the right decisions, the universe will reward you for it, and the right people will gravitate around you. Don't fall victim to heavy drinking like an overwhelming majority of police officers, don't fall victim to sleeping around or cheating on your spouse as many cops do, and don't be foolish enough to get yourself arrested - most importantly. Be a beacon of hope for the world and be a symbol of light. No matter what your chosen profession is, choose to be the best version of yourself in that profession and be a leader.

PART III
Preserving a Hard Earned Career

Chapter 13: Stay Healthy: Coordinate A Health & Fitness Program

In the previous chapter, I touched a bit on making sure that you're always training and always staying fit as a police officer. You have to have some kind of training program, and you have to stick to it. Even if you aren't a police officer, you have to stay physically fit in order to remain in proper equilibrium. If you are a physically fit individual who trains hard in the weight room and runs at least a mile per day, then you will become a far more efficient individual in all aspects of life. You must work out every day, or at least every other day, at the very minimum. You have to do whatever it takes to keep your mind healthy, and staying in shape is the best way to do that besides taking action on your goals.

Having a consistent workout schedule will decrease the likelihood of falling into temporary states of depression. It will allow you to be more present in your home life and more productive, and you will find yourself eating healthier as well. You are less likely to become a heavy drinker if you are constantly focusing on keeping your body in shape and, eventually, enjoying the results from the consistent hard work.

From when I was young and competing in cross country, soccer, basketball, baseball, and tennis, I was always in great shape because I held myself accountable. Today, I am still in great shape because I hold myself accountable. This is so important and vital to being successful. I included pictures in this book from when I was only 14 years old, 21 years old, and when I was 24 years old (in the process of writing this book). As you can see, I never lost the drive and self-discipline to stay in top physical condition. This is why I felt the need to include this chapter in this book.

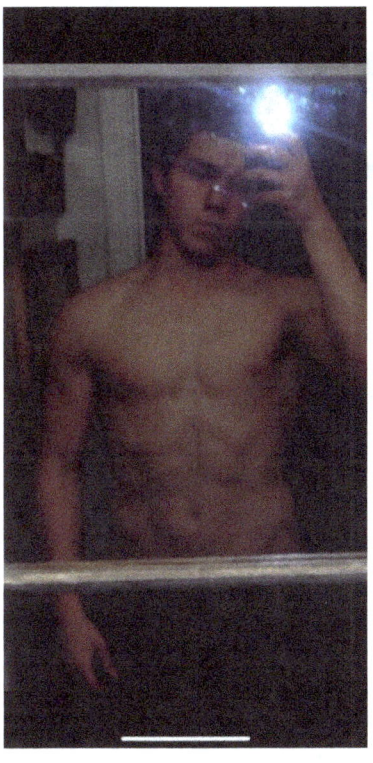
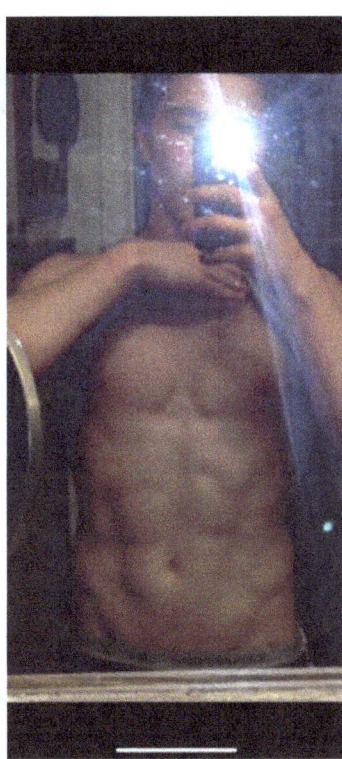

I myself, as stated earlier, have been like most police officers at one point or another in my career. You get done with a 12-hour shift, you take the uniform off, grab a beer from the refrigerator, and you start tipping a few back until you're feeling a nice buzz to relieve the stress of your shift while you kick back and watch "Better Call Saul" or "Breaking Bad" on Netflix. Other officers commonly go to the bar, which is, quite frankly, even worse, considering that it is against the law to consume alcohol and carry a firearm at the same time (at least in Michigan). Even if those officers aren't carrying while at the bar, just because they felt the need to drink. However, drinking is the worst way of easing the stress after a long night, and it only makes you fat, lethargic, dehydrated, smelling like the drink itself, and honestly - dumb.

Drinking does nothing good for you, and there have been proven studies to show it. It is a myth that consuming just one alcoholic beverage per day is good for you. That is proven in many studies to be utterly false. It has been proven that consuming zero alcohol is the best way to remain healthy and focused at all times. Absolutely nothing good comes from drinking. Drinking numbs your mind, decreases productivity, constricts your arteries, makes you reek of the unbearable scent of alcohol, and leaves you vulnerable and useless to those around you.

Think about it. When you are intoxicated on a Thursday night at 11:18 p.m., you can't lend a helping hand to someone when they call you for a ride home. What if it were an emergency? What if your kids weren't home and they had gotten into a car accident? How are you going to be able to get in your car and go pick them up unless you are willing to break the law and risk a D.U.I.

What if you are at home, and your mother or father is on their deathbed? They want you to come and visit them because they feel they don't have much time left. It's 2:00 a.m. in the morning on a Monday night. Your wife has also been drinking. You call your friends, but they are all drunk too. Nobody can pick you up, and there's not an Uber available. You can't go anywhere! You are stuck at home and can't visit your parents in the hospital when they need to see you personally. Why? Because you are drunk and have taken too many spirits. Why put yourself in such a position? Because you're sad? Exhausted? Angry? Tired? Enough with the excuses. Drinking is horrible for you, and it leaves you weak and vulnerable to the world's unpredictable events around you.

Instead of doing what others are doing because it is socially accepted and "cool," put down the beer can, bottle, a glass of whiskey, joint, vape pen, or other useless drug - and hit the gym. Start working on your physical body. Start perfecting your mind and making it a solid, bulletproof specimen. Start working on your book and telling your story. Start working on your e-commerce store. Start educating yourself and making phone calls to clinch a real estate deal.

Start planning out how it is that you are going to finally save up $50,000 and become rich.

Whether a cop or an everyday hero, do something that puts you on the map and frees yourself from the grasp of the Devil, who loves to see you drunk, high, discombobulated, foolish, numb, lazy, and powerless. Be better than the majority who pretend it is "cool" and "fun," and be a leader who demands the best of themselves and those around them. Do not accept anything that takes away from your personal development and spiritual clarity. Be the designated driver and be the one in control when no one else around you is. Be healthy, and be the wise one. It is better to be respected and admired for doing what is right than to be overlooked and accepted for doing what is wrong. It is far more admirable to be sober-minded and powerful than to be intoxicated and powerless. Why allow yourself to give up power over your life? Be disciplined, and be the person you would depend on if you were stuck in a ditch at 4:00 a.m.

When you are drained by the killers of alcohol or drugs, you're unable to clearly think through your problems in life, no matter how much you may disagree. Being a police officer, that should embarrass you that people can't depend on you because they know you're likely buzzed after your shift. Fuck that. Do not be that guy. Be angelic to those around you. Give them nothing to doubt about your character and values.

Drinking is a bad habit that many police officers get into because, for some reason, it has become a stereotype in many ways. They begin to drink just because their coworkers and friends drink. They follow the crowd instead of being leaders and taking the road less traveled. Better to be a leader who does what is prudent and wise than a follower who just wants to fit in.

I remember being in the police academy, and our PT instructor always warned us about staying in shape. We busted our asses, each of us losing about 10-20 pounds throughout the course of the academy. Those of us who could not run well (me being one of them) were all able to run 5 miles without stopping by the end of the entire police academy. We made it through the PT exit exam and succeeded through every day of Hellish PT evolutions and workouts. We pushed squad cars, flipped tractor tires, and did burpees until we puked. PT was Hell, but it made us solid and healthier human beings. This is why our PT instructor would be so adamant about staying in shape, so we didn't waste all the hard work. He warned us about how most police officers most commonly died due to traffic accidents and cardiovascular disease. Still, despite this harsh reality, I have seen so many police officers go from being in excellent physical condition during the police academy to fat and almost unrecognizable. Do not be this officer. If you are, then change it.

I was not the most physically fit person during my time in the police academy by any means. I was 220 pounds in my first academy and 240 pounds in my second academy. I want to make clear that I am not pretending to be the fittest cop that I have known because I definitely wasn't. As a matter of fact, despite being a college football and baseball player, a state championship powerlifter who placed 2nd and 3rd place in High School, a tennis player who competed in the Robinson tournament, as well as a cross country runner in middle school who placed top 10 in every race, I still was our worst runner. As mentioned earlier in this book, I remember middle-aged parents and 45 year old grandparents who were in better shape than I was. I was always at the back of the pack when it came to long-distance running. I was better at the strength and cardio workouts.

Today, I am 210 pounds, and I have never allowed myself to get out of shape. I am constantly training every day, even when I don't feel like it. I have always been this way throughout most of my life. When I was in high school, I would get through the day, and after the day ended, I would go straight to the weight room and lift. I worked hard even when I felt like shit because I always found that when I felt like shit, working out would make me feel good again. If I had a headache, lifting almost always took the headache away. If I had a stomach ache, lifting made my stomach feel better. There was never a better feeling than getting a new personal record every day, whether it was on the bench, squat rack, or deadlift.

I started lifting as an 8th grader, benching 165, squatting 225, and deadlifting only 265. By the time I was a senior competing in the state powerlifting meet, I was benching 310, squatting 485, and deadlifting 545. The reason I improved so greatly is that I was constantly pushing myself to new limits, and I never drank. I would eat two steaks a day, drink only infused water, constantly eat healthy breakfasts, and for dessert, I would only drink protein shakes. I was at the peak of my physical condition when I lived every day like this, and today, I still do. Even when I don't want to train, I force myself to do something, even if it's just running a mile or 100 push-ups before the day's end.

It is so important that whether you are a police officer, a doctor, a lawyer, a nurse, a teacher, a carpenter, a mechanic, an entrepreneur, or anything - you must train every single day. Never allow alcohol or drugs to enter your life, as these traits will dominate you and destroy your life before your very eyes. You will become slower, you will become dumber, less industrious, less motivated, and less present, and ultimately, you will take years off of your life. If you want to be a true leader and a true success, then you should always be sure that you are in excellent physical condition.

You should be able to run 2 miles without stopping. You should be eating healthy foods and consuming only healthy drinks on a daily basis. You should not be drinking any alcohol or taking drugs. I have seen too many fellow cops fall into the slavery of alcoholism and/or drug abuse. Refuse to be like the majority of people in the world. Be a leader and take care of your body. Respect the body that God has given you, and hold yourself accountable every day. Be better than you were yesterday physically, and you will surely be better mentally.

Chapter 14: Never Stop Learning - Be Industrious and Be Dynamic

Learning, and the enjoyment of obtaining knowledge, is a key trait of the wise. Being enterprising, studious, and strategic are the virtues of the highest earners, greatest negotiators, most successful business magnates, and most effective leaders. You have to be industrious and dynamic at all times in anything you pursue in life. When you finally become a police officer or when you retire from being a police officer, you have to continue learning. Even when I was a cop, I was constantly keeping myself apprised of the laws in my state. I was always reading books. I was studying psychology, real estate, e-commerce, private equity, cryptocurrency, finance, economics, engineering, and of course, writing. I was constantly working on side hustles. I was starting dropshipping stores, taking real estate classes to get my license, networking, DoorDashing, producing lousy music, working on my books, experimenting with blogs, creating automated YouTube channels, creating NFTs, buying gold, you name it. I was constantly doing anything I could to learn new markets and become a master in the arts by earning some form of passive income. I was always industrious and learning how to create new assets.

The learning never stops once you finally graduate from the police academy and pass the state exam. If you stop learning, then you will become just like the majority of people in today's society. They go to college, get a job or career, and work their way up the corporate ladder learning one thing - their job. In the 20 years they spend doing this, they are in constant fear of losing their jobs while only specializing in only one thing - their job. When they get home from work, they start drinking, switch on the television, maybe play some video games, go to the club, spend all their hard-earned money, buy stuff they like on Amazon, watch mindless TikToks, and then finally, go to sleep. Then, they repeat this process by worrying about one thing - their job. Don't be that person. Be industrious and be a forward thinker who has their hand in every cookie jar.

I remember a kid in my High School. Ironically, his name was Brendan, too, and even spelt the same. Brendan was more of a hustler than anyone I knew in High School. He had his own photography business, worked in the office for the school staff as an IT guy, and was even wiping down tables at our local bowling alley. While I was playing sports and making no money, the other Brendan was always making money and had multiple streams of income. Before anyone even knew what the word "lease" meant, the other Brendan had already leased his first car, and I remember it looking brand new. Everyone was impressed, but nobody was surprised because everyone knew that Brendan was the entrepreneur of our graduating class. This other Brendan was both industrious and dynamic, as well as diligent about his time. To this day, he is still very successful. I learned a lot from the other Brendan.

This goes back to earlier in the book, where I mention the importance of thinking like a business owner and having a minimum of 7 streams of income. Every millionaire has seven streams of income. Ideally, you should expand your creative mind and shoot for 20 different streams of income. You need to learn how to create assets, and above all else, you have to get used to creating a network. If you are an introvert, you need to strive to be an extrovert and crack out of your shell, as this was one of my greatest difficulties, not just in becoming an entrepreneur myself, but especially a police officer. People are amazing, and they are a resource. You have to be comfortable with communicating with people, and you have to be okay with getting out of your comfort zone in order to build strong, long-lasting relationships. In other words, you need to get comfortable with being uncomfortable.

If you can find a way to put yourself on the map, then you will absolutely be able to make more money and expand your network of other important people. You have to be dynamic in the process, strategic, and able to solve problems. This is where being a police officer helped me and gave me an edge. I learned to solve problems, and eventually, I learned to solve complex problems in the world outside of Law Enforcement. This is how to be industrious and dynamic. Being able to be industrious and dynamic will allow you to succeed in anything and outcompete your opponent every time. Solving problems, not being afraid to reach out to others for help, asking the right questions, and doing it with gusto and speed, make you dangerous and highly effective. As a police officer or entrepreneur, these skills are so important.

Chapter 15: Pay It Forward - Teach & Educate the Next Line of Warriors

To conclude this book, I end with an important chapter about becoming an educator and paying it forward for your fellow man. You don't have to be old and wise. You just have to have credentials and a proven track record of success in order to teach others how you did it. In today's world of hatred and fear, leaders are needed to educate the youth and pave the way for the generations to follow. You owe it to your fellow man to live a quality life so you can be a beacon of hope, a symbol of Triumph, and a testament to hard work and persistence. The reason I wrote this book was to educate people on my experiences as a cop and entrepreneur, mainly a cop. Becoming a police officer is not easy to do, no matter what anyone tells you. It's also expensive to become a police officer. It cost me around 7,000 dollars just to afford the academy I attended, including uniforms, gear, boots, and textbooks. If I could have done it again, I probably would have become a corrections officer first and then gotten sponsored to go to the academy as many of my other friends in the academy did. That would have been the smart move, but I wanted to waste no time. It was how I was going to graduate from college too, so it was the best way to get started as soon as possible.

Not only did I become a police officer, but I struggled to become one. I graduated from my first academy, failed the state exam twice too many times, redid the entire academy, graduated again, and then finally passed the state licensing exam separate from the academy. Before my time as a cop, I was a college student-athlete. Before that, I struggled to stay out of trouble and almost never even got into college. I played every sport you can think of, was exceptional at those sports, and that was my ultimate way into college. I cleaned up my act at the last minute and stopped hanging out with people who were going to get me in trouble. I worked my ass off and focused on accomplishing the goals my family believed I could achieve. Today, I am an author, entrepreneur, and public figure, all because of the adversity I worked through.

After all of my successes and failures, and once I had enough of them in my life, I realized that I was successful because of the failures. I never wanted people to make the mistakes I made along the way, so that is the reason I wrote this book. I want people to win. I know how to succeed and prosper through moments of adversity. This is the true way to succeed in anything. When I made enough money and became successful enough to write about it, that is exactly what I did. I'm not rich today, but I am pretty well off. I still live within my means. I started writing this book when I only had about six grand in my bank account. I was not wealthy before writing this book, but I still knew that I had to write about my experience as a police officer and how I got there because becoming a police officer is hard and worth writing about.

Life is hard in itself, but when you find a way to succeed through the trials and tribulations of life, you learn that you become stronger and more adaptable to the punches that life throws at you. You become wiser and more fit for any challenges that come your way. When you do it enough, eventually, you realize that you have to teach people how it's done. As I stated before - the world needs more great leaders who teach others how to win in the competitive arena of life.

The truth is, everyone has a story. Everyone has something they can teach someone. Every human being in the world has pushed hard and succeeded through moments of adversity and reached the other side of the tunnel to see the light at the end of it. But even with that known fact, people are still too afraid to show others how they did it, whether it be out of pride, ego, selfish desire, fear, or likely, all of the above. Everyone has a story, and everyone has an obligation to write it. Most never take the first step in even realizing they can.

I knew that I could provide value in this book. I knew I could teach others about not just my own experiences but real information on what it takes to accomplish what I have. I knew that from being a student-athlete my entire life and a police officer, I could provide everlasting value on how to not only become a police officer or entrepreneur but how to be successful in becoming one. Even as I write this book, starting from that six grand in my bank account and five grand worth of crypto investments, I quickly accumulated up to a 100 grand net worth from my investments and side hustles by the time I reached this exact point in the book.

I already know that I will become wealthy because I understand the game of wealth and business. I take time to learn the ever-changing rules of the game of business every day. I know how to sell, I know how to write, I know how to communicate, I know how to take calculated risks, I know how to lead, I know how to stay consistent, and I know how to provide value. If you can do all of these things, then you, too, will become wealthy. Becoming rich is not hard. It is a process, a metamorphosis, and a mindset. This is another subject I enjoy educating others on, as I have built many successful businesses, blown money, lost businesses, started new businesses, and learned from my mistakes. Again, this is another reason I am writing this book. I want to teach future generations about how to succeed in anything, whether it be becoming a police officer, a best-selling author, or an entrepreneur.

If there is anything I can leave you with, it's that nothing is ever easy. You can't expect anything to be easy. Everything is a challenge in its own way. What separates the winners from the losers are those who choose to quit and those who choose to keep going, no matter what the setback is. Most quit right before they reach the finish line, get the promotion, make the winning pitch, or get the "yes" from the investor. Most quit because the fear of failure overrides the excitement of winning. Most quit because their mind defeats them. They quit because they hate the feeling of temporary loss. Multimillionaires and other high achievers are very different. They do not shy away from temporary setbacks or taking risks. Their setbacks become their setups. To multimillionaires and highly effective people, every failure is another stroke to their ego, and they almost enjoy the failures as they create a more powerful story of success. Athletes are very much like this.

Athletes are the best when it comes to learning how to lose constructively. Overall, professional athletes have made their way to wealth and the highest levels of the game because they embrace failure and learn from each mistake they make, and they do it with gusto and swagger. They take criticism as a constructive resource so they can improve themselves and their craft. They use criticism to better understand their strengths and weaknesses while capitalizing on their mistakes and building upon them. This is why professional athletes find themselves becoming high earners. They outcompete their competition, but also, they never quit and better themselves every day. They practice no matter the storm, no matter the weather. This is why athletes oftentimes, even when not reaching the most professional levels, often find themselves in other high-paying careers. They often find themselves sharing the mindset of multimillionaires.

Multimillionaires are driven the same. They have learned from their mistakes and built upon them. They practice the basic principles of people who have obtained great wealth and success before them. Ray Dalio, the founder of Bridgewater, one of the most successful Hedge Funds on Earth, has written a book specifically called "Principles" because the principles of success are that important in any and all aspects of life. Wealthy people understand that business and life are like a chain link. There are strong links and weak links. Most people never try to strengthen their weak links, whatever they may be. They continue to build on the strong links, which is okay, but will not allow the chain link to be fully effective. Eventually, the weak links will break in life if not strengthened. This is a common principle that every multimillionaire or highly effective person knows.

Eventually, when you strengthen the chain of weak links in life or business, you will see success. At this time, it is when you have the choice of teaching others about your success and how you created your legacy or letting the opportunity pass you by. It is a disservice to not educate others on how you made your success. Although we live in a competitive world, leaders are not afraid to elevate the world around them. This is what creates a better world. This is where the "narcissist" or "selfish" altruist persona comes from. Do not be afraid to speak about the successes, and especially the failures of your life. People are interesting, and you are interesting, so therefore, you should tell the world how you are interesting and why. Be a leader, pay it forward, and like I am in this book, be the type who teaches the youth and future generations about how you reached success.

If you've made it this far, then congratulations. You just got smarter. You are one of the few who truly wanted to learn what it takes to become a police officer and how to become a successful entrepreneur. In reading this book, you learned about some of my life experiences as a police officer and aspiring entrepreneur. You learned about my story, my successes, and my failures. You learned what the job entails as a police officer, what other options there are if becoming a police officer is not in your interest, what is important and what isn't important during the struggle, what to expect in the police academy, the process of getting hired as a police officer, and how to keep the job as a police officer. You also learned the importance of becoming physically and mentally balanced, as well as how to think like a leader and educate the next generation when you have succeeded in becoming a police officer, entrepreneur, or anything.

Lastly, before you leave, remember one thing. Objectives that make you painful, sleepless, emotional, and restless - will all be worth every moment in the end. Never quit, never quitting. Thank you for reading or listening to this book, as it means a great deal to me that you are interested in potentially becoming a service to your community as a cop or as a business magnate. I wish you great luck in your journey, and be sure to never give up along the way. Be sure to read or listen to his book 2 or 3 times so that you can absorb as much value from this book as you can. Until next time, stay prudent, stay powerful, and stay wealthy. God Bless, and good luck in your journey.

Sent by the Gods
by Brendan Scott Ecker

Sent by the Gods, I win against all odds.

I stir the waters and rock the boat, but in the midst of chaos, I am both the calvary and the moat.

I see into the future and reflect on the past. To my visions, there is no enemy too great, too forged, or too fast.

I dine with Kings, walk with the common, and soar with the Eagles, though I am humble, I am dangerous to the forces of hatred and evil.

I watch the world mourn, as even I have fallen and been reborn, but what is more, I am fearless to knock at Satan's door.

I bleed, sweat, try, cry, and scream as my intensity and resilience are powerful beyond my dreams.

I fight, adapt, and endure, even when there is no sight of a distant shore.

I love, I ponder, and I jest, but make no mistake, I am only satisfied with the best.

You can put me to the test, you can think that I am less, but in the end, I will put your words to rest.

Nothing can break me, nothing can take me, and nothing can shake me - no matter the outcome, even my adversaries will thank me.

Though the wages of sin is death, regardless, I embrace the journey of living with each sunrise and each sunset.

I awaken with glee and gratitude, as the world is an enigma, and a miracle with each longitude and each latitude.

With each color, each creed, and each breed, there is only Greatness in humanity - and so I shall plant the seed, be valiant in great deeds, and build an empire of those who seek to Free.

I'm a warrior born to lead and a reason to believe.

So, therefore... I would rather die than fail to Succeed. There is no challenger, nor judge, nor jury, nor executioner more Powerful than Thee.